Paternoster Pocket Books No. 25

THE BONUS YEARS
A Positive Approach to Retirement

TITLES IN THIS SERIES:

THE "JESUS FAMILY" IN COMMUNIST CHINA
D. Vaughan Rees

THE HOUSEHOLD CHURCH
H. L. Ellison

STEEP ASCENT
Dorothy Dennison

THE ADVENTURES OF A DESERTER
Jan Overduin

BY WHAT AUTHORITY?
Bruce Shelley

WHAT ABOUT TONGUE-SPEAKING?
A. A. Hoekema

THE MYSTERY OF ISRAEL
H. L. Ellison

PHYSICIAN HEAL THYSELF
Dorothy Dennison

BLACK AND FREE
Tom Skinner

WORDS OF REVOLUTION
Tom Skinner

LIVING CHURCHES
John Williams

HOME BIBLE STUDIES
Derek B. Copley

HOLY SPIRIT BAPTISM
A. A. Hoekema

CHRISTIAN SCIENCE
A. A. Hoekema

JEHOVAH'S WITNESSES
A. A. Hoekema

MORMONISM
A. A. Hoekema

SEVENTH-DAY ADVENTISM
A. A. Hoekema

KIDNAPPED!
Eunice Diment

GET MOVING
Paul White

HERE COME THE GIRAFFES
Bob Bond

BUILDING WITH BANANAS
Derek and Nancy Copley

TO
MY WIFE
with whose
help and encouragement,
together with
that of family and friends,
this book has been written.

CONTENTS

PREFACE

The wise man in the Book of Ecclesiastes remarked that 'of making many books there is no end' and never has that saying been more apt than today as a glance at any bookseller's window will show. So much has been written on some topics that anything more would seem quite superfluous: but on retirement this is far from true for it is only now that the subject is beginning to receive the attention it merits. So I make no apologies for writing this book.

It is estimated that, with the general trend to earlier retirement, there will be within the next few years not fewer than ten million people in the United Kingdom who will have retired from normal working. Consequently, about one person in five will be living in retirement and, taking into account the increased expectation of life that modern medicine has brought, many of these will be able to look forward to a period of 15 to 20 years freed from the necessity of working for their living. These are the bare bones of a situation which we must be prepared to face as a nation and as individuals.

Before the coming of the National Pension Scheme, many of those who retired, having had little chance of saving any money during their working years, had to face the bleak prospect of subsisting on such help as their children, if they had any, could give or of having to depend on some sort of charitable aid. Life for the elderly, who had no means of their own on which to live or who had no family to look after them, was grim indeed. Many could only look forward with foreboding to ending their days in the workhouse, that dreadful and degrading form of public assistance which seemed to make poverty a crime. Fortunately, that has now changed for the better and, however inadequate we may still feel the level of the National Retirement Pension to be, the great majority of pensioners can look forward to a reasonable standard of living which, though it may not be as high as when they were earning full wages, is still vastly better than their grandparents had.

I can now look back on ten years of full-time retirement and they have been amongst the busiest, happiest and most satisfying of my life. Several years ago, I was discussing with a friend a project on which we were both engaged and which was taking up a great deal of my time. Seeing how much I was enjoying my retirement, and knowing how fully my time was occupied with various interests, he suggested that I should write a book about this subject so that I could share my experience with others and encourage them to make full use of their bonus years. At the time I was much too busy to make a start but now it is opportune for me to tackle the job.

By profession I was an engineer with down-to-earth experience on the shop floor as well as in design and management; I learned to use my hands as well as my head. So this has been written not as a theoretical study but as a simple, practical aid for other quite ordinary people like myself. There is an old saying that 'a pound of practice is worth a ton of theory' and this book is based on personal experience both in preparing for and in making full use of retirement. My aim is to encourage a more positive approach to the subject so that those who are reaching this stage in their lives may do so, not with forebodings but with keen anticipation of enjoying every minute of it. I am writing mainly for men because, as a mere man, I would not presume to suggest to women how they should use their retirement years. To the average man, the sudden break from his job, which usually has taken him away from his home each working day, comes as a shock. His main problem is to adjust himself to the new situation. If he has a wife, her problem is usually not her own retirement but her husband's. Her pattern of life will be comparatively unchanged and her home will continue to be her chief preoccupation: but she will not like the prospect of having her husband under her feet all the day with little to do. They both wonder how he is going to fill his day usefully. So, if this book helps to solve this problem for some husbands, it may go a long way towards solving their wives' problems as well. On the other hand, there is much common ground to both the sexes in retirement over matters such as pensions, accommodation and other matters, so I hope this book may prove useful also to those women who have to face life on their own when they too have to give up their jobs.

Being a committed Christian, it is inevitable that my attitude to life should be based on the faith which has been from my youth, and will continue to be, the mainspring of my life. In many ways, as will be evident from this book, this has deeply affected my outlook and interests and I am convinced that it has greatly helped me in my approach to the problems of retirement and old age. My interests are not all specifically Christian or church-based but extend into many fields and I want this book to be helpful to all, regardless of creed or circumstances, who have to grapple with the problems of retirement. Many others, besides myself, have proved that it can be a period of real enjoyment and fulfilment; so please read on and see how you too can come to regard the final phase as *The Bonus Years*.

JOHN CANSDALE

1
55 LOOKS AT 65

Hear counsel and receive instruction that thou mayest be wise in thy latter end. (Proverbs 19:20)

Ten years before I was due to retire I did something rather strange. I wrote a letter to myself! I sealed it in an envelope marked 'To be opened only on retirement' and it was put away with my will and other important papers. When the time came, I opened it and read with great interest what I had written to myself ten years before. There is nothing magic about the ten year period but I have always maintained that the 'old' person is someone who is ten years or more older than yourself! This seems to hold true throughout life. The twenty year old thinks that anyone over thirty already has one foot in the grave! So I found it instructive and amusing to look at myself at 65 from the viewpoint of my younger self. Recently I have read the letter again, as it suggested I should, and even after twenty years there is still nothing that I would disagree with, though I think I could add quite a lot to it! It was the reading of this letter that finally made me decide to start on this book; so perhaps it would not be out of place to put it in here and let you read it too.

March 1959

My dear John,

I want you to read this letter on the day that you retire and after that to read it at intervals to remind you of much that you will have forgotten as you get older. And if you, like your father, reach your 80's, please read it often for it should help you and those with whom you may be living at the time.

Old age comes upon us so gradually that many of us fail to realize that we are no longer young. We tend to let time move past us while we stay put. 'Times change', we say, and the inference is that we do not! Alas, this is often only too true! The insidious effects of age are seldom apparent to those who are old; but they are only too obvious to those who are young, or should I perhaps say, younger. I am writing this just before my 55th birthday and I am still young enough, I hope, to be able to understand the impatience of youth and the intransigence of old age. Young people lack the experience that brings full understanding but old folk have travelled so far from their youth that they have often forgotten much of what they learned on the way. Youth and age are poles apart in many things but they are alike in that they are impatient and intolerant with each other.

Here are some of the practical points of daily living, some of the do's and don'ts for you to think about and I sincerely hope that you will allow yourself to be guided by them. You will certainly be easier to live with and your useful life will be extended further into old age if only you will allow yourself to profit by the mistakes of other people. Maybe no one has told them what not to do and they have forgotten that, when they were younger, they swore that they would not be like the old folk who had bothered them.

Don't imagine that you are indispensable! No one ever is. The world will carry on after you have gone much the same as before. But you can make it easier for those who have to carry on if you give them a chance to get ready before you go. Don't hold on to work that younger ones are willing and able to do, and which they often can do much better than you can. It is a tragic thing to see an old man clinging to a job that, obvious to all but himself, he should have passed over to a younger man long ago. Be alert to see when you are losing your grip and encourage someone younger to take over the reins.

There is work for older men to do and it is more likely to come to them if they are wise enough to give youth the chance to take the lead. Never grudge giving up something that you have done for more years than you can remember. If that is so then it is quite time that you did give it up so that some fresh life can come into it.

Never criticize unless your opinion is asked. And even then remember that times do change even if you do not and what was accepted in your youth may not do for today. Try to keep clear before you the fundamental principles of life, the eternal values that are abiding, and keep your mind open on the non-essentials, for example the sort of clothes we wear. Your grandchildren will certainly dress very differently from the way you dressed as a boy. Why worry?

As with criticism, so with advice. Never give it unless you are asked. And this particularly applies to your own children and their familes. Grandparents are notorious for either spoiling or scolding. Avoid both! If your children's children are to be brought up then it is their parents' job and not yours. They will do it quite as well as you did, and possibly better if you did your job properly when you were training them. Don't compare the way your grandchildren behave with the way you think you remember your children behaved. Distance lends enchantment to the view and the rose-coloured spectacles that grandparents wear often look back to the 'perfect' children of long ago. There never were, and there never will be, such children!

Avoid having favourites amongst your grandchildren. They will spot it in a minute and you will cause a lot of trouble in the family if you do not treat them all exactly alike.

If it is humanly possible, avoid living with, or very near, your children. They will appreciate you all the more for an occasional visit rather than having you on top of them all the time. They have their own lives to live and are perfectly capable of doing so. And if it ever does become necessary to live with one of them, do make sure that you arrange to go away for regular periods more than once a year if you can. They need the relief of being on their own just occasionally, however much they love you.

With old age comes increasing leisure and you can so very easily forget that younger folk are still in the hurly burly of life. A busy mother has little time to sit and chat with grandma: a business man has a full day's work to do and may often be away in the evening on business of some sort. He may appear to you to neglect his garden but remember that you have all day for yours and he may get but a few hours at the weekend, and then have all the other household repairs to do as well. You can help, if you are on the spot, but do remember that he has as little time to spare as you had at his age.

And speaking of gardening, do not expect always

to be able to do the same as you did when you were young. Then, a hard day's digging did you good and you enjoyed it, or pretended that you did!. But now, if you do too much you will suffer for it and it will be your own silly fault. Don't expect pity when you do foolish things! There is no point in being a martyr when a little care would have saved you, and others, a lot of trouble.

You cannot stop your body getting old but you can try to keep young in spirit and in outlook. It is no use trying to force your presence on young people. The Youth Fellowship quite rightly restricts membership to the under 30's. But they may like you to come sometimes to talk to them; the more so if you have maintained a youthful approach and show that you do try to understand them. They will value the wisdom that the years have brought to you. Talk directly to them; don't talk down to them as though they were a bunch of kids.

Now for some even more practical and personal points which are only too obvious to us as we observe some of the old folk about us today. Your sight will not improve with age so please do wear your glasses when washing up or preparing the vegetables. It may not matter so much when you are in your own home; but even there your visitors will notice the egg marks on the 'clean' plates and the dirt in the cabbage! It is more important when you are staying with your children or elsewhere. It is quite natural that you will want to help with the washing up, though it may not be appreciated in someone else's kitchen; but, if you do, please make sure that it is impeccable. Otherwise your daughter may be forced to do what we have so often done and that is to go over all the plates again when grandma, or grandpa, has gone up to bed! Your help may have given no satisfaction to anyone but yourself.

When you have retired from business, there will no longer be the urge to keep spruce and well-dressed: so there will be a tendency to get slack over personal appearance. Slovenly habits come so easily with old age and we can lose not only our self respect but our friends as well.

Loneliness is so often an accompaniment of old age and this has its real dangers. Perhaps the greatest is, strangely enough, talkativeness. It is the not unnatural reaction after being alone but it can be very trying to relatives and friends if you not only monopolise the conversation but also hang on to them when they are dying to go. And never outstay your welcome when your host would much rather have your room than your company. You must watch yourself carefully over this for the talkative person never realizes what a bore he really is.

Keep your mind alert. Look, listen and read so that you maintain a wide range of interests and are able to converse on topics beyond your garden and your house. You will probably have aches and pains for there are few old people who are spared such things; but no one is wanting to hear about them and others will think more of you if you keep them to yourself.

Just one word about money. The amount you leave is really of minor importance so use what you have wisely and well while you can. Your children's needs, after they have homes of their own, are probably greatest when their children are small, before they have been able to save much or establish themselves in good jobs. Then is the time when your help can be most useful; more so than by leaving it to them in your will, for by then their needs may not be nearly as great.

One closing word which I am sure I have no need to remind you about. There is a wonderful promise in Isaiah 40:31:

> But they who wait for the Lord shall renew their
> strength,
> they shall mount up with wings like eagles,
> they shall run and not be weary,
> they shall walk and not faint.

So, whether in youth we fly with eager wings, or, in the prime of life, we run with patience the race set before us, or, as we near the end of the journey, we walk, maybe with halting steps, towards the final goal, the source of our strength is ever the same. Our waiting is upon One who is the same yesterday, today and for ever.

Doubtless there is much more that I could have said. But this is, I hope, enough to be a help along the way. This is yourself now speaking to yourself across the years, maybe 10 or 20 or 30 years from now. The advice comes from an age which is intermediate between your eldest son's age and your father's, a vantage point that is worthy of your consideration, even though, when you come to read it, you may say, 'What was I thinking about to write that!'

Your own self,

JOHN.

2
LOOKING FORWARD TO RETIREMENT

Be Prepared (The Scouts' Motto)

Baden Powell's good advice to those who were at the start of their careers is equally applicable to those who are ending them and facing retirement. There are still all too many who come to this important stage in their lives without having made any preparation for it. Forced retirement is a term which is normally associated with those who have to give up their jobs prematurely because of ill health or for other causes beyond their control. It could well be applied to many who retire at the normal age but who do so with the greatest reluctance because they want to continue working. Some are so immersed in their jobs that they cannot imagine what life would be like without them. Such men 'live for their work' and when that comes to an end there is little left to live for. It may be due to a selfless devotion to duty, with which it is difficult to find fault, but it is often associated with an urge to make money or hold on to power. Whatever the motive may be for this clinging attitude to their jobs, retirement finds them quite unprepared.

Professor W J H Butterfield of Cambridge wrote this in a letter to the Daily Telegraph on the subject of retirement: 'In the medical profession, we are constantly meeting cases where, once the work pattern is removed, the will to live likewise disappears. Indeed some of my colleagues have been tempted to insert "sudden death retirement syndrome" as the cause of death in certificates where no other medical reason can be isolated. We know far too little about the stress that retirement places on those who are unprepared for it . . .'

We have not yet fully emerged from the period when to go on working was normal and necessary until the infirmities of old age made it impossible to continue. There was no recognized retirement age nor was there any provision for any pension for the majority of workers. When the Old Age pension was introduced in Britain in 1908, it was given only to those who were over 70 and, even then, pensioners were subject to a means test before they could claim their 5/- a week. So, few saw any need to prepare for retirement; the end of a working life was virtually synonymous with the end of life itself.

In 1928, when the Contributory Pension Scheme was introduced, the retirement age was set for men at 65 and for women at 60 and so it remains today, though with the current urge for sex equality, it is felt by many that this is an anomaly that should be corrected. There is now a growing tendency towards earlier retirement and many jobs offer voluntary retirement at any time after 60. This trend is being accelerated by the unemployment situation which seems likely to be a permanent feature of modern life and which is bringing about many changes in our attitudes to work.

The consequences of these changes are apparent in our thinking about retirement and the need to prepare for what may be a lengthy period is increasingly being recognized. Much is being done now to help those who are having to face this major change of life.

In considering what can be done by way of preparation, there are two quite different aspects to bear in mind, the long term and the short term views. There is a sense in which every stage of life is a preparation for the next stage and the man of 65 is the product of all his preceding years. The old saying is true, 'The child is father to the man'. However sudden the break from his job may be, a man cannot break away from himself; his thinking, his whole attitude to life, will be basically the same the day after he retires as it was the day before. Ideally, therefore, preparation should start in youth when the foundations of a man's outlook and personality are being laid down. I am not suggesting that a young man, immersed in his first job, should start to plan what he is going to do when he retires. But he should realize that what he is, and what he does, when he is 20 will have a bearing on what he is and does after he is 65.

It is reasonable that a man's job, whatever it may be, should be his main interest. After all, it is his livelihood; his well-being and that of his family will depend on it. However, in contrast to earlier days when a man's job demanded nearly all his time and energy and when a 60-hour working week was not unusual, the steadily shortening working week now leaves much leisure time for the average man. How this time is spent is left almost entirely to individual choice and it can be usefully or otherwise employed. It is the opportunities that this greater leisure provides that should help a man to prepare for the fuller leisure of his retirement. It should enable him to develop that wide spectrum of interests which make for a full life both before and after 65. I am fully convinced from my own observation and experience that a man with a wide variety of interests outside his job comes to his work with a freshness and vision that are often lacking in the man whose sole interest is in his job. In subsequent chapters I shall be referring to many of these outside interests and the time to cultivate them is not just before retirement but throughout the working life.

It may seem rather unfair, in a book that is directed to those who have retired or are about to do so, that I should stress this point about a lifetime of preparation. Is it not too late to start to think about this matter at 65, or even at 60? I think not! It is never too early to start; but it is also never too late to mend! Even if, only at that late stage, the need to have a wide range of interests is appreciated, then something can be done about it. Of course, it will not be easy for a man who has lived entirely for his job suddenly to diversify his interests and to occupy himself in other ways. It can be done and it is surprising what latent talent there is in most men which can develop once it has been given some encouragement. For example, I have several friends who, after retiring, have attended art classes and have discovered an ability to paint pictures which had never been suspected. Skills such as this can be put to good use even though not many can hope to become as famous as the American folk artist, Grandma Moses, who started painting when she was over 60.

So much for the long-term aspects of preparation. Fortunate indeed are those who approach retirement with that variety of interests which will make them remark, as so many have done, that they can not think they ever found time to go to work!

The short-term aspect of preparation has come much to the fore in recent years and help is available in a number of different ways for those willing to accept it. Many industrial concerns are now taking pains to prepare their employees for retirement, recognizing that this is part of their social responsibility towards those who have given loyal service often for many years. The Rubery Owen Engineering Group were pioneers in this field 30 years ago and much credit for this is due to the head of the firm, the late Sir Alfred Owen, who was well known for his wide philanthropic and religious interests.

The present Rubery Owen scheme provides a pre-retirement course for male employees at the age of 50, and for female employees at the age of 45, so it recognizes the importance of preparing in good time. It consists of a series cf evening lectures and discussions culminating in a full week-end conference. Attendance is voluntary and costs the employee nothing. Three main subjects are covered – finance, health and leisure activities. The aim of the course is to encourage those who are within 15 years of their retirement to look ahead and to plan their future in such a way that they can approach retirement with pleasure rather than with fear. A further course of a similar nature is provided for men when they reach 64 and for women at 59, when they are much closer to the actual time of leaving. In addition to the various company schemes, courses are being run by many local education authorities and by the Workers' Educational Association. These may take the form of day release, afternoon release, evening or residential courses. Co-ordination of much of this work is being done by the Pre-

Retirement Association which is sponsoring and encouraging courses on an increasing scale throughout the country. The PRA offers 'Approach to Retirement' kits, covering a selection of Government leaflets, PRA publications *etc*. dealing with all aspects of retirement. Details of these can be obtained by writing to the PRA. The association also publishes an excellent monthly magazine, called *Choice*. This provides not only interesting reading but contains valuable information on all aspects of retirement. A subscription to this magazine, some years before the time comes to retire, could make a useful contribution to the process of preparation.

I have been taken to task sometimes when speaking about retirement if I have used the term *planning for retirement*. To some people, the word 'planning' savours of bureaucracy and government interference and this is something they want nothing to do with once they are their own masters. They have had enough of planning in their jobs. So I prefer to use the term *preparation for retirement* and, whilst some are obviously more ready for it than others, we all need to look ahead to those days when there will be no one to tell us what to do. The whole purpose of preparation, whether by the formal courses or by your own thought and study, is to help to develop the positive approach to the matter. You will not be told what you *must* do, but what you *can* do. The choice is wide; the opportunities are many; the decision is yours.

3
GOOD HEALTH

Health and fitness are better than any gold, and bodily vigour than boundless prosperity.
(Ecclesiasticus 30:15)

It is well to remember that health is much more than just physical fitness: it has been aptly defined as 'a state of complete physical, mental and social well-being.' So, ranking high on the list of prime requirements for a happy and long retirement is that of good health. Compared with this, adequate income, suitable accommodation, absorbing interests and many other factors, important as they may be in the overall picture, are secondary. This has been borne out by a recent competition in the retirement magazine, *Choice*. Contestants were asked to place in order of importance five ingredients for a successful retirement and the majority of those who entered the contest put good health in first place. It is interesting to note that the judges had placed it third in the list! I feel therefore that there is good reason for dealing with this subject first of all, and at some length.

Of the various aspects of health, the mental is of primary importance for, to a large extent, it conditions the physical. This is particularly noticeable right at the start of retirement which is a critical stage psychologically since it involves for most people a complete change of life; and it is the mental attitude to this change which is vital. If there is a negative approach which views with resentment having to give up the work of a lifetime and is apprehensive of a future which could be without purpose, then the physical results can be disastrous. Without a purpose in life and a will to live, many have succumbed soon after retirement and have never even begun to enjoy it. On the other hand, a positive approach to retirement and to the possibilities that it offers can provide a zest for life which is the essence of good health.

During our early years, we all take our physical health for granted; and without conscious effort to keep fit we eat our food, exercise our bodies and experience the joy of living. Only if something goes wrong and pain or discomfort makes us conscious of our bodies and their failings do we turn to the doctor for help. But, as we grow older, bodily ailments become a more familiar part of life and we no longer take good health for granted. Even then it is significant that those who are most concerned with their aches and pains are usually those who have least to do and so have more time to think about themselves. Hence the importance of a positive attitude to life and a wide range of interests in retirement to form a foundation for good health. This positive attitude also involves our self image. Some people, even though they would scorn to be considered elderly, see themselves as fragile and treat themselves almost like hothouse plants. By such extreme carefulness they may succeed in extending their lives slightly but at the expense of the fulfilment and freedom that others enjoy who care less for themselves and more for other people.

The over-cautious are more likely to rust out than to wear out, which is surely the preferable hazard.

Much ill health in the modern world is due to what are often called 'stress illnesses' and these take on a variety of different forms. The pressures and problems of life today are very great at all levels and the man with many worries in his job may look forward eagerly to the day when he can leave them all behind him. I must confess that, when I sometimes meet old colleagues who are still battling with industrial problems, I am very glad to be out of it all. But it is a mistake to think that retirement has no problems and that our worries cease automatically at 65. The man who is prone to worry will never lack scope for it at any age and the problems of his work can easily be replaced by other worries over finance or accommodation, and even more, over health. Good health involves both mind and body and the influence of mind over matter is nowhere more obvious than in this field.

A Healthy Life

What are the different factors that affect health in retirement? Let us consider some of them.

Ageing

Old age is a relative term and means something quite different to the 20 year old and to the 60 year old. For many it has a rather unfortunate connotation with undertones of decrepitude, and it is interesting to note that in many countries, efforts have been made to get away from the words 'old people'.

We have terms such as *senior citizen* or *members of the third age group*. Even so, those of us who are over 60 and who come into this category should not resent such titles since it is a fact of life that we are all getting older every day. The process started before we were born! It is a fact also that some people are old before their time whilst others are perpetually young, at least in outlook. There is much truth in the saying 'You are as old as you feel'. This applies more perhaps to the mental than to the physical state and we have to accept that, as we grow older, changes are taking place in our bodies. This ageing process affects us all and we have to try to understand it and live with it. Science has made great strides in recent years but it has not yet discovered the secret of perpetual youth though many wish it would. Whether the cosmetics industry would welcome such a find is rather doubtful!

The body is like a machine, a very wonderful machine when compared with anything that man can make, but in the course of time some parts do begin to deteriorate. The muscles gradually lose their suppleness and the joints begin to stiffen; the heart, that marvellous little pump, finds it harder to push the blood through arteries that are continuing to harden; the eyes can no longer adapt to the full range of vision required and spectacles are needed to help them; and so we could go on through all the other bodily functions. The body does in time begin to wear out but it is a mistake to assume from this that old age and ill health necessarily go together. It is possible for robust good health to continue well into old age and with proper care there is no reason why this should not be more general than it is. My own father came to live with us when he was 85 and for five years he found occupation and much pleasure in helping to run our very large garden. Then we had to move North and he went into an old people's home where he was active well into his nineties. He finally passed away, still active in mind, though not in body, in his 102nd year.

This process of ageing is something over which we have little or no control. We can no more hold back the march of time than King Canute was able to stop the onrush of the waves. But, had he accepted the fact that the tide was coming in regardless of his wishes, he need not have got his feet wet! So we must accept ageing but not ill health.

It is sometimes said that good health is a gift of the gods, that some are lucky and some are not. It is true that some are blessed with a strong constitution inherited from their parents and that others, through no fault of their own, always seem to be ill. However, it is equally true that many of the ills from which we suffer are self-inflicted and that, to a very great extent, our health is under our own control. Good health in retirement is not just a matter of luck: it depends very much on our life style during the preceding years as well as the way we live in our retirement. So, let us consider some of these aspects of health where it is very much up to us and where a healthy life is the product of a healthy life style.

Diet

It has been said that more people commit suicide with the fork than with any other weapon! Overeating is one of the great dangers in the affluent society of our times and it is a sad reflection that one third of the world's population eat too much whilst the other two-thirds are underfed. As a social evil this is most deplorable but it does not end there. Overeating leads to obesity and this becomes a serious health hazard for those concerned. The over 60's are particularly vulnerable as the risk of illness due to overweight increases with age. A good retirement motto would be 'Eat less and live longer'.

The body needs to take in food to provide energy in the same way that an engine needs fuel to keep it operating. The foods which produce energy are the carbohydrates, which are usually taken in the form of starches and sugars, prominent among them being the various flour products and potatoes. The amount of fuel needed, usually referred to in terms of the number of calories, varies according to the shape and size of the body and the amount of energy to be expended. A man doing a heavy navvying job will naturally require more than one who sits at a desk all day. For the same reason the amount of energy-producing food needed by those who are older and less active will not be as much as for younger people.

There is also a continuing need for protein, to replace and renew the ever-changing body and this is provided by such foods as milk, milk products, eggs, meat and fish. Wholemeal bread, soya flour, nuts and other vegetarian foods provide further protein. Also essential are vitamins, some of these coming from fresh fruit and vegetables which should form part of a balanced diet. As we get older, our bones start to get weaker and more brittle and unless there is an adequate intake of calcium and of Vitamin D, the chief sources of which are milk products and margarine, they are likely to collapse under any unusual strain. Also, to maintain good health, small quantities of certain salts and minerals are needed and these are provided quite adequately by a good mixed diet. Roughage, such as is provided by root vegetables and the bran in wholewheat products, should form part of a well-balanced diet to ensure good digestion and elimination. Water is also essential and three pints or more, in some form or other, should be taken every day.

An excellent book, full of information on the subject of diet, is published by the Consumers' Association entitled, *Which? Slimming Guide*.

It is obvious that we must eat to live: but that is not the same as saying that we must live to eat! *Enough is Enough* is the title of a book by John Taylor, Bishop of Winchester, in which he pleads for a simpler life style in the face of the desperate world situation and this phrase might well be applied to our eating. Not only does it make sense in terms of conservation of the world's resources, and a more equal sharing of them, but it is sound sense for the individual as well. When the intake of calories exceeds that which the body needs to provide the energy which has to be expended then the surplus turns to fat. This is the natural reaction of the body to surplus food. Little harm would be done if the overeating of one day were balanced by a fast on the following day but many people so love their food that they overeat regularly without realizing that they are not increasing their energy but their weight. The tendency to put on weight does vary from one individual to another and there are certain illnesses, and certain treatments, which cause obesity. Also there are a few fortunate folk who are able to eat what they like yet who never seem to put on weight. But for most of us, especially after retirement, the danger of getting too fat is very real and the only answer is moderation in our eating. For the maintenance of good health, weight watching should be given a high priority. Statistics show that the death rate increases by 13% for every 10% that an individual is overweight compared with the average for his build.

How often the doctor's first words to an elderly patient are, 'You must lose some weight!' He may be able to give some pills that will help to suppress the appetite but it is usually a matter of deliberately cutting down on the intake of fattening foods. This means reducing the amount of bread, sugar and potatoes and similar foods and also fats of all kinds such as butter and cream which have a very high calorific value. To cut down on sweet cakes, confectionery, sugar in the tea and other luxuries involves a considerable effort of will but it really is the only way to get and keep the weight down. A weight-reducing diet need not be dull if more emphasis is placed on the protein foods like meat and fish, milk and cheese, with plenty of fresh vegetables and fruit. To those with limited means this may seem like a counsel of perfection, for these are often the more expensive foods and require more preparation than the fattening foods. This is where the skill of the housewife and of the gardener can be given full scope so that a sensible non-fattening diet can be made as exciting and appetising as fish and chips! To be brutally frank, it must be pointed out that if you are overweight the probability is that you have been eating more than you need and you could cut down the size of your meals without in any way losing energy. You will be all the better for it in weight and health – and in pocket.

Retirement does give more opportunities to study this question of diet. There is more time for the preparation of interesting meals that do not add weight and there is no longer the need to buy those expensive 'convenience' foods that appeal so much to the woman who has to go out to work and run a home as well. The cheaper cuts of meat can, with care and thought, be made really appetising and nourishing. It is surprising how much good meat there is on a pig's head and, if you have a dog to feed, as we have, nothing is thrown away except the bones! Many people bake their own wholemeal bread too and the only trouble is that it is often so much nicer than shop bread that it takes a lot of strength of will not to eat too much of it! Brown bread, whether homemade or from the bakers, is so much better than white bread in maintaining good health.

Exercise

Just as there is a widespread tendency to eat too much so there is a corresponding, and consequent, tendency to exercise too little. The motor car has a lot to answer for! Daily exercise for both body and mind is essential for good health. The danger in retirement is that the easier pace of life encourages us to get slack in these things. Instead of the daily rush to work we can take our time over everything we do and go at our own pace however slow. It is all the more important that the walk to the station in the morning and back at night, or the cycle ride to work that some take, which ceases abruptly on retirement, should be replaced with an equivalent in physical exercise. This is essential to maintain muscle tone, to promote good circulation, to aid digestion and to encourage sound sleep. When we were young, exercise came naturally to us; now, those of us who are grandparents marvel at the way our grandchildren manage to 'keep on the go' from morning till night, and we are content to watch them from our armchairs. Active sports like football and athletics are for the young and most of us who are older must be content with gentler exercises. There are some folk who manage to enjoy quite strenuous sports like tennis or cycling well past retirement age and, if you are in the habit of doing this sort of thing, then it is excellent if you can continue with it as long as possible. Before taking up any unaccustomed form of exercise it would be wise to check up with your doctor that you can safely undertake it. Jogging is a popular exercise for many to-day but it should be undertaken with caution by anyone past middle age. Before breakfast exercises may be appropriate and necessary for those who have to dash off to work but elderly muscles which have not been used during the night are least ready for any vigorous and sustained physical effort. Take regular exercise but take it easy!

The easiest exercise, and the cheapest, is undoubtedly walking; and this can be indulged in whether you live in the town or the country and all the year round. I have a lively beagle dog who insists on taking me out for a walk twice a day without fail and this is good for both of us. It is better to walk two miles a day regularly than to do just one long walk once a week. Never set out on a strenuous walking holiday unless you are in training for it; it could do you more harm than good. Swimming is excellent exercise for anybody living within reach of a swimming bath or near the sea. A friend of mine who is over 80 still swims in the sea regularly during the summer months despite having two artificial hip joints. Golf provides exercise for arms and legs and is a sociable sport but it is not for everyone. Gardening is probably one of the best ways of keeping fit as it provides exercise for every part of the body and is productive as well. Take care not to overdo it: a sudden burst of heavy digging, if you are unaccustomed to it, will probably leave you with that 'every picture tells a story' look.

Even if the above forms of exercise do not appeal to you, or if you are housebound, there is still scope within the home for following some of the radio keep fit exercises. Nor is there any lack of instruction books which provide all sorts of helpful exercises for those who can only do them in their own homes. The important thing about physical exercise is that it must be kept going regularly if you are to benefit from it.

It is equally important that the mind should be exercised. Too many men, who for years have had jobs that have kept their minds constantly at a stretch, suddenly find that they have only the concerns of home and garden to occupy them. For a while, the relief from pressures at work may be a welcome change; but the mind, like the body, needs exercise to keep fit and it must not be allowed to stagnate. This question of mental activity has much to do with purposeful activities, a subject which I shall be dealing with in a later chapter. It is encouraging to remember that, although at 65 physical powers are well past their peak, mental powers are not. The brain can be as keen, even if not quite as quick, at 65 as at 35. Wisdom and knowledge can both increase with age up to a point which is usually well beyond retirement if only the mind is kept fully exercised. A machine that is not used can rust up and become useless; and this is also true of the mind.

Relaxation

Exercise and relaxation could be considered as opposite sides of the same coin; both are essential for good health. I am using the term here in the more technical and medical sense of the releasing of tensions, both emotional and physical. We live in a world where there are tensions at every level and not only at the top, though they may well be worse up there. Tensions in the office, the shop or the factory reflect in the home and the family and, even when the tensions are not between individuals, they may be within the individual himself. How often it has to be said of someone, 'He never seems able to relax!' Many of the ills in society today are the outcome of the tensions that exist – between management and labour, blacks and whites, rich and poor and, alas, also in the home between husband and wife, parents and children. Relationships become strained as tensions build up and can be restored only when the tensions have been released. A simple analogy is that of a steel spring. It has to be designed for a particular job and as long as it is not stressed beyond the safe limit for which it has been made it will fulfil its task indefinitely. If it is overstrained beyond that limit then it will first become deformed and ultimately it will break. For all of us, life brings some tensions and, within our limits, which will vary from one individual to another, such tensions can be tolerated and indeed are a necessary part of life. Our existence would be very dull if we were not constantly being challenged to press on, to improve our performance, to reach greater heights of achievement. If pressures or tensions (the analogy of the spring holds good for both) build up beyond the safe limit, permanent damage can result and ultimately there will be a complete breakdown. Many of the large number of mental breakdowns that occur come in this way and they are a tragic feature of modern life. More often than not a breakdown begins with some emotional tension and this in turn results in bodily tensions and even serious illness. Insomnia, headache, and even sickness can have their origin in some emotional state though the subsequent physical symptoms are real enough. To get rid of our tensions, we must relax. But how?

We hear a great deal about the practice of Yoga and of various forms of meditation, mostly connected with Eastern religions. Some of the physical exercises of Yoga can be helpful for body relaxation and are soundly based. Personally, I have not needed to use such methods but it is interesting that they all place much emphasis on the relaxation of both body and mind. It is this aspect that doubtless accounts for their popularity in these days of so much stress and strain. Nature has provided one of the best means of relaxation in sleep but unfortunately when tensions build up this often fails; worries and insomnia too often go together. Many seek relief in tobacco, or alcohol, or other drugs and the huge output of tranquillizers is evidence of modern man's search for release from his tensions. Such relief is never more than temporary for these things are only palliatives and do not cure.

Volumes could be, and probably have been, written on this subject but let me tell you what has for me been the chief source of relaxation from the tensions of life. From my youth I have had a simple Christian faith out of which has come the experience of prayer and communion with God. As a lad of 16, I had a long journey to work which involved an hour in the train and I learned to use that time to read my Bible and to pray. A train may seem a strange place for meditation but, as I had to leave my home at 6.15 am, the journey provided the time and opportunity for me to gain strength for the long day ahead. This habit of early rising and of having a quiet time with my Bible and in prayer has continued with me and become an essential part of my life, even in retirement. Stresses and strains are part of our common lot but only those who have experienced the tension-releasing power of prayer can truly understand its value. It is not, as some seem to think, the prerogative of great saints and holy men, using those terms in the popular sense, to meditate and pray: it is the birthright of every true Christian. Here is the promise written in Paul's letter to the Philippians: 'Don't worry about anything; instead, pray about everything; tell God your needs and don't forget to thank Him for His answers. If you do this, you will experience God's peace, which is far more wonderful than the human mind can understand. His peace will keep your thoughts and your hearts quiet and at rest as you trust in Christ Jesus' (Philippians 4:6,7 – Living Bible). Is there any better recipe for peace than this?

Using the term relaxation in its broader sense it

can be found in music, drama or reading. Radio or television, used with discrimination, can also provide relaxation from the problems of life by diverting the mind from its immediate troubles. It all helps with the process of 'unwinding' which is very necessary to avoid the build-up to breaking point. Some can find relaxation in hobbies and pastimes which are usually far removed from the daily job and they rest the mind because of the complete change they bring. I used to find that an hour or two in my workshop at home in the evening provided just the relaxation I needed after a trying day at my office desk. If life for you has been so busy that you have never had time to relax, then retirement offers you the opportunity you have not had before. So, get busy and learn to relax!

Sleep

The ability to sleep soundly and to awake refreshed is one of life's greatest blessings and it should be enjoyed by all who are healthy and live normal active lives. 'Sweet is the sleep of the labourer whether he eats little or much.' So says the Preacher in Ecclesiastes 5:12. There is sound sense in this: the person who has had a busy day with mind and body active is much more likely to sleep soundly than someone who has had nothing to do. Yet it is a fact that sleeplessness is all too common a problem especially for the elderly. There is no simple remedy for insomnia; it depends on so many different factors. Methods of inducing sleep are legion but what is effective with one person is not necessarily suitable for another. Pain of any kind can prevent sleep as also can worry and if there are tensions in the mind, the body cannot relax in the way it needs to for sound sleep.

Continued sleeplessness is not natural and there is usually a cause for it, so it is wise to seek for medical help. Sleeping pills are useful in the short term but should not be permitted to become a habit; but they may help to restore a normal sleeping pattern which continues after they are stopped. After 65, we need to remember that our need of sleep, as well as our ability to sleep, does diminish as we grow older. Provided we are refreshed by our sleep it does not really matter how long, or short, it is. People's needs vary. Some can still get up at 6.0 a.m. after a lifetime of practice while others find they must go to bed earlier or rise later. Some fortunate folk can take a nap at any time and awake refreshed after quite a short time. John Wesley, in his very strenuous life of travelling and preaching was renowned for this as also was Sir Winston Churchill. Some find that a short midday sleep can help to recharge their energy but often this does not appeal to those who have led active lives!

My own recipe for sound, refreshing sleep, based on my own experience would be this:

Spend the day in useful and interesting occupation of mind and body, exercising both to the limit of your ability.

Make sure you have a comfortable bed, sufficient bedclothes and, in winter a sure means of warming the room and the bed before you retire.

Retire with mind and body fully relaxed. Try not to take your worries to bed with you!

The last thing my wife and I do before getting into bed is to read together from *Daily Light*, which is a well-known selection of scriptural texts. This has been our regular nightcap for more than forty years. There is no better way both to start the day, and to end it, than to read God's word and to pray.

Smoking

Although I have never smoked, I used to keep a box of cigarettes in my office desk so that I could offer them to visitors. This I continued to do for many years until a member of my staff, who was a heavy cigarette smoker, became ill and died from lung cancer. I visited him many times during his illness and observed his steadily deteriorating condition. Towards the end, the dreadful struggle he had to breathe was heart-rending to watch. After that experience I swore never again to offer a cigarette to anyone.

It never ceases to amaze me, now that the link between smoking and lung cancer, as well as other respiratory diseases, has been so firmly established, that so many continue this habit which is bad both for their health and their pocket. I know that many feel that the comfort that tobacco brings is worth the risk involved; and that many smokers do live to a ripe old age. But there is no doubt that the risk is there even for the moderate smoker and, although cancer may be avoided, the effect on the lungs and heart is always harmful. The latest figures show that about 50,000 premature deaths due to smoking occur every year in the United Kingdom. I know many who have given up smoking, and even though it must have been a very hard struggle to break the habit of many years, they now find themselves so much better in health that they never want to smoke again.

There was a time when to be a non-smoker was to be exceptional but, fortunately, attitudes have changed and the non-smoker is no longer considered peculiar. I have often had the remark made to me, 'How lucky you are never to have smoked!' No doubt this does make it easy for me to advise others to stop smoking but ask any doctor, even if he smokes himself, and invariably his advice will be, 'Give it up!'

Alcohol

I find this rather a difficult subject to write about for I realize that, as distinct from smoking, it is the abuse of alcohol, rather than its use, that constitutes the danger and the evil. As a lifetime teetotaller, and having seen some of the tragic consequences of alcoholism amongst men with whom I have worked, and, more recently, amongst those I meet in my prison visiting, it would be natural for me to take a strong line against taking alcohol in any form. But I have many friends who drink in moderation without any apparent ill effect on their health and who do not seem to be in any danger of ever becoming slaves to drink. It would not be reasonable for me to suggest to them that they should become total abstainers like myself and I must leave the matter as one where each individual must make his own choice. The question of expense is one that cannot be ignored, especially by pensioners, many of whom are unlikely to have much to spare on unnecessary luxuries. It can also become a form of masculine selfishness where the husband indulges himself at the local pub to the detriment of his wife and the housekeeping money.

It is well to remember that the alcoholic probably started as an occasional or moderate drinker and never intended to become addicted to it. The connection between drinking and road accidents is well proved, hence the advice that is now given to all motorists, 'Don't drink and drive!' We may well see some restrictions placed on drink advertising of the same kind as are now applied to tobacco advertising.

I believe that the advice of Paul in Romans 14:20, 21 is relevant in this as in other matters where our conduct may affect others. He wrote, 'Everything is indeed clean but it is wrong for anyone to make others fall by what he eats; it is right not to eat meat or drink wine, or do anything that makes your brother stumble;' Having been involved in youth work all my life, and being only too aware of the danger of alcoholism amongst young people, I have felt that for the sake of example, if for no other reason, I have been right to abstain.

A Healthy Body

So much for those matters which are largely under our control, attention to which will play a great part in maintaining a good state of health. Our life style does have an important bearing on both the quality and the length of our lives. However, due to the natural process of ageing, or possibly due to some inherited or acquired weaknesses, there are certain other matters which will affect our health and which are not under our control in the same way. These too form part of the total health picture and need to be considered.

The Heart

The heart is the nearest approach to perpetual motion that we are ever likely to experience. From its first faint beat in the womb to the final flutter before death it never stops. I know that it is just possible for it to stop for a brief period and to be started again but for most of us our hearts go on pumping blood around our bodies every moment of our lives. The heart never stops but it does, due to ageing, lose some of its power as we know only too well if, when we get older, we indulge in too vigorous exercise. Grandparents cannot compete with their grandchildren on the flat, and even less uphill!

Although the heart itself is sometimes the source of heart failure, it is more often the arteries through which the blood is pumped that are the main cause of trouble and hardening of the arteries is part of the process of ageing. The extent to which animal fats are harmful by raising the cholesterol level in the body and in clogging the arteries is still a subject for medical debate; but it is a fact that a high fat diet has an extremely high calorie content and as a cause of obesity is dangerous and should be avoided.

The fear of heart failure is very real from middle age onwards for it seems to happen so often and it is usually sudden and unexpected. It should be of some comfort to those who have retired to know that the chances of a heart attack are less after 65 than during the preceding 20 years. The usual form of heart attack is that of a coronary thrombosis in which a clot of blood formed in an artery restricts the flow of blood to the heart. Such an attack is usually not fatal and many patients recover and are able to lead reasonably normal lives afterwards.

Only in severe cases is prolonged rest required and the tendency now is to encourage gentle exercise so as to speed up recovery.

Another anxiety amongst elderly people concerns high blood pressure. Some increase in blood pressure as we grow older is necessary in order to pump the blood through narrowing arteries so this in itself need not cause alarm. Your doctor can readily check your blood pressure and will advise treatment if he considers it too high. If you worry about blood pressure then it will probably go even higher! The condition is frequently associated with obesity which is not surprising when you consider the extra work that this imposes on the heart.

A third fear for many is the possibility of a stroke, with the loss of speech and the paralysis that often accompanies it. Strictly speaking, this has only a remote connection with the heart for it is caused by the bursting of a blood vessel in the brain, or by the formation of a blood clot which cuts off the supply of blood to the brain. Here again modern methods of treatment can deal with the trouble and minimise the consequences.

Heart transplants are still in the experimental stage and most of us will have to be content with our own hearts for as long as they will do their job. There is no reason why they should not serve us well provided we treat them sensibly by careful diet, regular exercise and the avoidance of smoking.

Lungs

Diseases of the lungs are common in the elderly and recovery from coughs and colds does take longer, especially in winter time. Bronchitis and similar ailments become more troublesome, particularly in those who smoke. Shallow breathing is a common failing but it is possible by a sustained effort of will to get into the habit of breathing deeply all the time. This can be developed by exercises and there are a number of books which go into this in great detail. It is a cheap but effective method and improves the health generally as well as strengthening the lungs.

As we get older, our body's vital systems slow down and the temperature control mechanism becomes much less efficient. With the slower circulation, heat is not so evenly distributed about the body and a warm environment is essential. The air temperature should not be below 18 degrees Centigrade (65 degrees Fahrenheit) as it is air that goes into the lungs; cold air cools the lungs and causes pneumonia.

Central heating is a great comfort to those who find keeping warm a problem. The ideal is to have enough background heating to maintain a reasonable temperature day and night throughout the living and sleeping rooms. Cold bedrooms and windows open to the frosty air may be good for budding Arctic explorers but they are bad for old people. The electric blanket, which we may have scorned when we were younger, can be a great comfort when we get older. A word of warning, however, is necessary here as, by warming the skin, the peripheral blood circulation will increase, so impairing the body's heat retaining mechanism. So the electric blanket is not a substitute for a warm bedroom: you need both for maximum comfort and health. Remember, if the underblanket type is used it must be switched off before you get into bed but the overblanket type can be left on all night and it is usually designed with a control that can be adjusted to give just the amount of heat needed to keep the body warm. This type is advisable if there is any danger of incontinence. All blankets should be tested regularly to ensure that they are safe electrically.

It is a tragedy that even in this country there are many cases each winter of deaths from hypothermia where people die due to their body temperature falling to a dangerously low level because of lack of warmth. Genuine poverty is often the cause but not always. A heating allowance is given to people suffering from many medical conditions, and one need not be in receipt of Supplementary Benefit to receive this help. Your doctor or health visitor can advise you about this.

Joints

'My rheumatism is real bad!' This is a remark which we naturally associate with some old person sitting in a chair, unable to move about due to stiffness and pain in the joints. Few of us, as we get older, can expect to escape some discomfort due to the fact that wear and tear, if nothing worse, affect our joints and muscles. Rheumatism is the popular word applied to such ills, but the medical term covering the common joint afflictions of retired people is 'the degenerative arthroses'. The ankles, knees, hips and spine are particularly prone to be affected, and if one or more joints become acutely swollen and painful, the patient is said to be suffering from 'arthritis' of that joint. Not only is pain a problem which may interfere with sleep, but stiffness and difficulty in moving about may result. Sufferers will confirm that it may take up to half an hour to loosen up each morning, before being able to walk even as far as the bathroom. The pain and the stiffness can usually be helped by aspirin, or other drugs may be prescribed by the doctor. Heat treatment, such as heat pads or infra-red lamps (not ultra-violet), is often very helpful. Why not suggest one of these when asked what you want for a Christmas present?

In cases of serious joint damage, replacement joints can now be fitted and this method has been outstandingly successful with the hips. Methods of dealing with joint troubles by medication, physiotherapy and surgery are constantly being improved and your doctor will know what is needed to deal with your particular trouble. The importance of regular exercise as long as you can keep it up cannot be over-emphasized; joints that are not used can become unusable.

Eyes

Deterioration of sight is a normal part of the process of ageing and few of us reach retirement without finding it necessary to use spectacles at least for reading. We soon come to accept this appendage to our face as part of ourselves and would feel lost and helpless without it. The job of glasses is to restore our sight, as far as possible to normal for all purposes, hence the frequent need for bi-focal lenses, or separate spectacles for reading and for long distance work. Regular testing of the eyes every two or three years, preferably by a qualified optician, will enable your glasses to be changed if necessary and will also show up any disease that may need treatment.

Cataract is quite a common condition and although there may be a considerable loss of sight during the period leading up to the time when it can be removed, there is every prospect of almost full recovery of sight afterwards.

Too many people continue to use spectacles which are no longer suitable for their eyes and endure, quite unnecessarily, poor vision which new lenses could greatly improve. New ones can be obtained under the National Health Service at a reasonable cost and they are provided free for those who are eligible for Supplementary Benefit or have an income below a certain level.

It is most unwise to use spectacles other than those which have been tailored for you. The chances of someone else's lenses suiting you are remote and they could do harm to your eyes. Sight is something too precious to take any chances with. When it begins to fail, it becomes increasingly important to have good lighting in the home and the need for this is often overlooked. A light of the right type and intensity, conveniently sited, can make all the difference to the enjoyment of reading or working. Even with the present high cost of electric power, the difference in running cost between a 60 watt and a 100 watt bulb is quite small but may well eliminate the eye strain consequent on using a poor light. The fluorescent tube may not be suitable for every room but for the kitchen or work room it is ideal and it gives more light for less cost compared with the normal tungsten bulb. It is also important to have adequate lighting on landings and staircases, with convenient switches so that they can be put on at all times when it is necessary for you to see where you are going. This is a safeguard against accidents to which we become increasingly prone as we get older. Most accidents in the home could be avoided if proper precautions were taken beforehand.

Ears

It is strange that, whilst the wearing of glasses is quite normal and socially acceptable, with the frames often designed to be ornamental, the use of hearing aids is still considered to be peculiar and every effort is made to render them small and inconspicuous. Yet deterioration of sight and hearing are alike part of the normal process of ageing for most people. Deafness is often a worse handicap than blindness in that it creates greater isolation; the deaf person is often not recognized and accepted as the blind person is. The danger with deafness is that the sufferer tends to withdraw into himself because he feels so cut off from others and this can lead to psychological difficulties. When he is unable to hear what others are saying, it is easy to imagine that they are talking about him and this can engender a persecution complex. We need to be alert to deafness in others and to take care to speak directly to them with clear enunciation of every word; and we can only hope that others will do the same for us if the need arises.

If hearing does become a problem, it is wise, as a first move, to make sure that the trouble is not due to wax in the ear. A thorough syringing by a doctor or nurse will quickly effect an improvement if this is the cause. There are a variety of hearing aids now available and these can help certain forms of deafness but not all deafness can be relieved in this way. Expert advice may be obtained through your doctor who will refer you for testing to the ear, nose and throat department of the local hospital. Never be persuaded to buy a hearing aid until expert medical advice has been obtained as to what is suitable in your particular case. Regular checks are needed to ensure that the aid continues to be suitable for you. Retired people are now eligible for behind-the-ear hearing aids and these are probably superior to most commercial aids, as well as being freely supplied and maintained.

Teeth

It is a regrettable fact of modern life that a good set of teeth is a rarity and few reach retirement without having to wear a denture. The damage to teeth is often done in childhood so it is rather too late at 65 to do much about it. Such teeth as you have should be treasured and thorough, daily brushing is essential to minimise further decay. Likewise a regular visit to the dentist, preferably every six months, will enable him to maintain the teeth in good condition as long as possible. New dentures may be necessary from time to time, not only to replace teeth that have had to be extracted, but to adjust to changes in the mouth that come with age. New dentures can be obtained through the National Health Service at a very reasonable cost compared with what you would have to pay privately.

Sometimes dentures become loose and difficult to keep in place and this is a common problem with the very old. Dental fixatives, usually in the form of powder to dust on the plate before putting it in the mouth, can be helpful but the best plan is to have new ones fitted. Many people shrink from what is often a long and painful process of 'breaking in' new dental plates and I have known some who have kept their new teeth for use only when they had visitors! It is rare for new dentures not to feel strange at first and much patience and persistence is required before you can wear them with comfort. In my own experience, new dentures nearly always require some adjustment before they can be used with comfort. It may be necessary to go back to the dentist several times before they are quite right and even then persistence is needed to go on using them until you are hardly conscious that they are there.

Feet

It is not only from the elderly that we hear the remark, 'My feet are killing me!' It would be more correct in most cases to blame the shoes for the trouble rather than the feet. I write feelingly on this subject for I have to wear a surgical shoe on one foot because that leg is shorter than the other due to an accident when I was a young man. Unless that special shoe is a really good fit, I have difficulty in getting about but if it is right I can walk well.

Foot trouble is often caused by wearing shoes not for the good of the feet but for the appearance of the user. The damage has often been done in early years and the resulting trouble with corns, bunions and such like shows up later and can seriously restrict mobility. The immediate remedy for any foot trouble is to be sought from the chiropodist and in many places special facilities, and prices, or even free treatment, are available for pensioners. Details of these can be obtained through your doctor. The chiropodist can not only deal with the immediate trouble but will advise regarding suitable footwear to minimize further problems. Some find it necessary to have a regular appointment for treatment and this may well be worth while.

Foot trouble is accentuated if you are overweight for this imposes an overload on the feet and naturally they start to complain. So this is a further reason for weight watching!

The feet are designed for walking and not for operating the pedals of a motor car, nor does this provide the exercise they need to keep them fit. So the rule for trouble-free feet is to wear comfortable shoes and to wear them out – walking!

Bowels and Bladder

The elimination of the waste products after the body has extracted what it needs from the food and drink that has been taken in should be easy and natural; and for those in good health this is normally so. But, with increasing age, problems do arise and chief amongst these is constipation. There is often a real fear that if there is not a daily bowel movement something is wrong and laxatives are in great demand. Normal bowel function varies widely from one individual to another; from once or twice a day to once or twice a week. Purgatives taken regularly can be harmful and it is much better to rely on regular exercise and a sensible diet. This should include roughage, whole wheat products or bran, fresh fruit, vegetables and plenty of fluid.

Difficulty in passing water is fairly common amongst men as they grow older and one of the main causes of this is enlargement of the prostrate gland. This can be dealt with, when the doctor decides it is necessary, by modern surgical methods and it is now considered a comparatively minor operation for anyone in reasonable health.

Persistent trouble with the bowels or the bladder should not be allowed to continue without seeking medical help, especially if there is any trace of blood in the water or the stools.

Sexual Activity

Sexual needs vary very greatly with different individuals and tend to diminish with age. They may cease altogether with some married couples, particularly if, for one reason or another (snoring is a good example!) they occupy separate beds or even separate rooms. On the other hand, some will want to continue the physical pleasure of sleeping together and find mutual fulfilment in sexual intercourse until quite late in life. It must be stressed that individual needs and desires vary widely and what may be perfectly normal for one couple may be quite otherwise with others. It is to be hoped that husband and wife, long before retirement, will have learned to adapt mutually to each other's needs. In this, as in every other part of married life, respect and unselfish love for each other should be the ruling factors if success and happiness are to be achieved and maintained. As with those who are accustomed to regular physical exercise, so with sexual activity, the effort involved is not dangerous in any way and the fear that it may bring on a heart attack is quite unfounded.

When Should You Stop Driving a Car?

I suppose many car drivers, if faced with this question, would reply, 'Only when I'm refused a car insurance or a driving licence.' This throws the onus on the insurance companies and the doctor who examines the motorist on their behalf, assuming they decide that such an examination is necessary: or on the driving examiner who carries out the driving test which can be required in certain circumstances when the driving licence has to be renewed after the age of 70.

But there is more to it than that and we all ought to ask ourselves the question before we reach the stage where someone has to tell us to stop. It is not only the car driver who is at risk but the other road users, motorists and pedestrians, as well.

It is often claimed that the elderly motorists are less liable to accidents because they drive fewer miles and often limit themselves to the daylight hours for driving. This overlooks the fact that with the advancing years not only do the senses of sight and hearing lose their sharpness but the reaction time is considerably increased; and all this comes about without our being conscious of the gradual deterioration. Maybe we drive more carefully, more slowly and further from the kerb but this can all irritate the impatient driver who may overtake in a dangerous situation; the accident which follows will be put down to his recklessness but the 'careful' driver will have contributed to it even though he will not be blamed.

How then are we to judge when, for our own sakes as well as for others, we should give up driving a car? Sometimes it is forced upon us when, for example, an acute illness, such as a stroke, has impaired the use of a limb and it becomes physically impossible to drive. But in many cases it is very hard for the doctor to draw the line and to say positively to his patient, 'Don't drive!' There are certain medical conditions such as epilepsy, diabetes and 'black-outs' which result in impaired consciousness where your doctor will advise you not to drive. Also anyone taking any form of drugs should not drive without obtaining the permission of the doctor prescribing them.

There are strict requirements for eyesight before a driving licence is issued and any deterioration, other than a temporary one, affecting the sight must be reported to the licensing authority immediately. If the sight of one eye is lost for any reason then the stereopic vision is also lost and this can seriously affect driving ability, particularly in anyone who is elderly. This would be a good reason for giving up driving.

Even though the car does become for so many a vital part of life so that having to manage without it could be a serious handicap, it is best to be realistic about it and to give up driving before an accident happens. If both husband and wife drive, then one or other will probably be able to carry on at least for a time so the car can be kept in use.

Treat your doctor as a friend and if he advises you to stop driving then listen to him and do not argue about it. You may have driven for forty years without an accident but he is anxious that you should not have one today or tomorrow.

When You Are Ill

If you are able to lead a healthy life and maintain a healthy body then your need of a doctor will be minimal and there are many retired people whose proud boast is that they never trouble their doctor. The less we have to call for medical help the better it is for us, and for the doctor! However, there are few of us who do not have occasion, if only infrequently, to seek the expert help that our medical services can provide.

The National Health Service in Britain makes its facilities available on the basis of contributions paid up to the statutory retirement age. Men of 65, and women of 60, are entitled to free prescriptions merely by signing on the back of the prescription form. Some payment is still required for such things as new spectacles and for dental treatment and dentures but even these charges are remitted in the case of those who are entitled to Supplementary Benefit.

Various aids for the severely handicapped such as wheel chairs, artificial limbs and hearing aids can be obtained free through the Health Service and for the housebound there are other services available such as home helps and meals on wheels. Those who retire before reaching the statutory age should consult their local office of the Department of Health and Social Security as to their entitlement under the Health Service for such benefits as sick pay.

The setting up of Community Health Councils in the United Kingdom is a recent move whereby local community interests can be represented in the operation and development of the National Health Service. This will give the customer a voice in its affairs. A leaflet will be available at local hospitals giving the address of the area CHC, together with the names and addresses of its members who will be widely representative of the area. Each council will have a small staff who will be available to give advice and guidance and you can, if you wish, make a direct approach to your local member. The CHCs are open to receive suggestions and complaints on any matters connected with the Health Service.

Your Doctor

The advent of group practices, health centres and clinics has meant that the era of the family doctor is passing. We have to accept this as inevitable with the rapid development of medical science, the specialization of skills and the multiplication of facilities. Many will regret the passing of the one who was so often the friend and confidant of the whole family and whose sympathy and understanding was probably as effective as his physic in keeping us well. This loss of personal touch is regrettable for it had a value for the individual patient that does not exist in the crowded waiting rooms of the specialist clinics of the hospitals, or even in the medical centres of the group practices. This is unavoidable as different individuals are involved at almost every stage and diagnosis now seems to depend more on the machine than the man. Fortunately we are not yet completely at the mercy of the machine and the computer whose function is to supplement the work of the doctor and he is still human like ourselves. Fortunately, also, there are still many G.P.'s who do carry on the traditions of the good family doctor as far as is possible in the circumstances of to-day.

A cordial doctor/patient relationship is vital, especially in the later years in life and fortunate indeed are those who have been able to establish such a link with their doctor over a period of years and do not need to change. Those who move away to a new area, as so many do in retirement, have to face the problem of choosing a new doctor. The choice should not be delayed until the need for him arises as that is not the time to start looking around. An important practical point is to pick a doctor who has a clinic or consulting room within easy reach of your home. It is not always convenient to use a car, even if you have one, and the time may come when you are unable to use it; to be able to walk to the surgery is a great advantage. But it is equally important to find a doctor with whom you feel you can establish a good relationship and in whom you have confidence. Talking this over with others in the neighbourhood, and particularly with your local chemist, can be helpful and they will be able to advise you as to suitable doctors. In this way you can get a general idea of the local doctors and there will usually be some choice even though for practical reasons it may not be large.

In Britain, under the National Health Service, you are free to choose, or even to change, your doctor but you must remember that he too has the right to accept or refuse you. So, if you are moving away to a new home, make sure you register with a new doctor as soon as possible so that he can obtain your medical file from your old doctor. He will then be able to refer to this when it comes to your needing any treatment. Once you have a new doctor, even though you may feel that he is not as good as the old one, do follow his advice, take the remedies he prescribes and give him full co-operation. If the medicine does not suit you, go back and tell him about it. Don't throw it away and then complain that it has not cured you. Consult him whenever it is necessary even though it is never easy to decide just when this actual stage has been reached. Above all, never stay away from the doctor because you are afraid that he may discover something seriously wrong, such as cancer. Even this, if dealt with at an early stage, can be treated and often cured. You are more likely to die from neglect on your part than on the part of the doctor!

Private Medicine

Whilst there is an obligation on the part of all of us in Britain to pay National Insurance contributions, it is not incumbent on us to use the facilities that are available under the Health Service unless we wish to do so. That the great majority of people do use the 'free' health service is obvious but those who can afford to pay separately for private medical treatment are quite at liberty to do so.

There are a number of provident schemes, such as BUPA, which offer benefits ranging from payments during illness or when in hospital to full cover for private consultations, operations and treatment in hospitals or nursing homes. They are all forms of medical insurance and as such the benefits are naturally dependent on the premium that is paid and this is assessed according to the age at which one joins the scheme, very much as it is with life assurance policies. Those who are in one of the schemes before retirement may well like to continue with it afterwards as the likelihood of benefitting from it increases with the age of the patient. It is doubtful however if it would be worthwhile joining a scheme for the first time after retirement as the premium would be rather high and some organizations impose an age limit beyond which you cannot join.

Private medicine is attractive in that it does offer certain advantages such as more leisurely consultations by the specialist of your choice and, sometimes, speedier treatment than could be obtained under the National Health Service. It is this aspect which raises some of the moral issues over which there has been so much debate. Despite considerable opposition to all forms of private medicine, it seems likely that they will continue to operate, possibly in complete independence of the N.H.S., so long as there is a demand for them and money available to pay for the service. Doctors and specialists may at some future date be forced into a situation where they will have to opt for either the N.H.S. or private practice and will not be able, as at present, to operate in both fields. Whether the patient will be forced into the same position remains to be seen but at the moment he is free to continue as an N.H.S. patient under his own general practitioner and at the same time to consult a specialist privately or have treatment in a private hospital, provided he is willing to pay for it.

My wife and I have had considerable experience of doctors and hospitals under the N.H.S. and, whilst we would not claim they were perfect, we doubt whether we would have had better or more considerate treatment if it had all been carried out privately. There is some advantage in having a private room immediately after an operation but, in the later stages, and in most cases these days that means within quite a short time, a general ward has a great deal to offer in the way of companionship and interest. What is even more important, there will always be someone in it who is in a much worse state than yourself!

A Final Word

You may feel that it is presumptuous of me, being an engineer and not a medical man, to tackle this important subject of health. It is such a vital matter in retirement that it could not be left out so I have tried to write in simple language about some of the matters involved in enjoying a healthy life after retirement. I have drawn on my own experience, observation and reading; and I am much indebted to my son-in-law, who is a doctor, and to others, for vetting this chapter and for advice on the more technical points. Much of it will seem to be rather elementary and mere common sense, but it is surprising what misunderstanding there is on some of the basic issues and a reminder of the simple principles of healthy living may not be out of place in a book which sets out to encourage others to get much more enjoyment out of their retirement years.

4
THE RETIREMENT HOME – WHERE AND WHAT?

Happy the man, whose wish or care
A few paternal acres bound,
Content to breathe his native air
In his own ground.
(Alexander Pope)

This idyllic picture, in Pope's eighteenth century poem on solitude, may seem rather out of place today, when building land is so expensive and houses are being put up eight or more to the acre. But it does remind us of the sort of vision that many people have of the peaceful home they would like to live in during their retirement. They may fancy a little cottage in the country, or a bungalow by the sea, or even one of those exotic villas in Spain. It is a subject, and a very important one, that should be given careful thought well before retirement actually comes. The decision about it will depend on the circumstances of each particular case and no hard and fast rules can be laid down. It is a personal decision and should be made only after every relevant factor has been taken into consideration. The first thing to think about is obviously the location.

Where?

For many, this presents no problem. They have lived in a particular area for years, possibly for the whole of their lives; their family and friends are all around them and their roots are well established in that place; it is clearly the right decision to stay put. Anywhere else would be a mistake and that's an end of the matter.

For others, there is no such simple solution. The mobility of labour which is so common today means that moving around is something to be expected as part of the price to be paid for promotion and advancement. Local roots do not get down very deep before there is another move. It means that children, when they grow up, more often than not move away for their training and then for their jobs so that members of a family are often very widely scattered. So, where are you going to find that 'ideal home'? There are three main factors to be considered.

Family and Friends

If you have children, and possibly grandchildren, you will not want to live too far away from them. It can be a mistake to move in next door, for they must be allowed to have independent lives, but it can also be a mistake to live too far away from them. Grandparents can have much joy in their grandchildren, and vice versa, especially if they live at the seaside! Even for single people, or couples without children, the nearness of other members of their family is usually a factor of importance. To move away from all your friends and to settle down in a new district where you know nobody can prove a bad start to retirement unless you are of the type who quickly makes new friends. It is easy to take your friends for granted and to realize how important a part of life they are only after you have lost them. My wife and I moved away from Manchester where after ten years we had many good friends, and retired to Weymouth where we had none. There were good reasons for making this move but we certainly missed our friends. Fortunately, by joining a friendly church, we quickly found a new circle of friends, and we have never regretted the move. Nor have we lost all our old friends for, living near the sea and keeping an open house, visitors from all parts drop in to see us and often come to stay so that in the summer time our spare room is seldom empty. Many others, like ourselves, have proved that a move right away to a new home can be successful; but weigh it up very carefully before you decide that it is right for you.

Facilities

Remember that you will be living in your new home all the year round, in the winter as well as in the summer. The house that looked so attractive in the sunshine of August may have quite a different look on a bleak day in January. How convenient a location is it going to be in terms of daily living? How far away are the shops and the post office where you can collect your pension? Is there a convenient bus service close at hand? Even if you have a car you may not always be able to use it, and some alternative is most desirable. How hilly is the district? You may enjoy hill climbing when you are 65 but will it be as easy in ten years' time? And what about a church within reasonable distance where you can find a spiritual home? It is sad to find some church members who take great care over their choice of a retirement home but forget to think about a church until afterwards.

What about being able to continue with your major interests? For the woman it may be the Women's Institute, the Mothers' Union, or a favourite charity. And for the man it may be golf, or football or a particular hobby. The facilities for continuing your interests after retirement are a vital factor in choosing a place to live in.

The question of health is another aspect that is equally important. If you suffer from a particular ailment, it would be wise to enquire how the climate of the place is likely to affect it. Always aim for a locality which will improve your health. Generally speaking, the South of England offers a milder climate than the North, and this is why large numbers of retired folk congregate along the South Coast and in the West Country. But North Wales, the Lake District and the moors of Yorkshire also have their attractions and many find happy retirement there. When you choose the place in which to live, let it be your head rather than your emotions that makes the final decision.

Finance

Almost inevitably your income will take a drop when you retire so you will need to assess the costs involved in moving to a new place and of living there. House prices tend to be higher in the popular retirement areas and living costs, particularly in the seaside towns, are usually greater than in the industrial areas and in some of the large cities. Rates vary a good deal and these need to be taken into account as well as the price of the house. Additional cost is involved in selling one house and buying another, and the distance over which your belongings will have to be moved will determine that further cost. Moving from a larger house to a small one or to a flat may help, but the higher level of prices in the new district may easily cancel this out.

If you have been renting your house, then the availability of rented accommodation in the new area may be the deciding factor unless you are in a position to consider purchasing a property.

For those who are fortunate enough to have finance available, another course is open. They could invest some time previously in a property in the place where they plan to retire. It may then be possible to let this for part of the year, but to reserve it for holiday and other visits. This enables the owners to try out the area and to put down some roots before actually settling down in retirement.

Retirement abroad

With so many people now taking continental holidays, the attractions of the sunny Costa Brava and other Mediterranean resorts encourage some to retire to the sun and leave behind the British winters. There is no lack of enticing advertisements seeking to persuade people to purchase villas or apartments in areas where they can enjoy their retirement in warmth and sunshine all the year round. If you have no ties or if you need to live in a more equable climate for your health's sake, then it might be worth it and there are those who have made such a move successfully. It does mean cutting yourself off from family and friends in another land where you will be residing for twelve months in the year and not just for a brief holiday. If you do consider doing this, make sure you deal only through reputable channels, for some people have become involved with unscrupulous property developers and have found their dream houses turn out to be only castles in the air. Before making any decision, check the regulations over the transfer of any money, the payment of your pension, the local health facilities, and especially any continuing liability you may have for payment of UK taxes.

What?

Some will have as simple an answer to this question of the sort of house they want to live in as to its location. They have a house where they have lived for years amongst their family and friends; it meets their requirements for a retirement home, so there is no earthly reason why they should uproot themselves and move away. Those who find themselves in this fortunate position are a minority. Most people, even if they stay in the same locality, find that some change of house is necessary on retirement. The house you have been living in, whether you own it or rent it, may be too large and too expensive, so you have to find something smaller and cheaper. If it is large enough to convert into two flats then this is a method of reducing the size and increasing your income at the same time by letting the other half. Quite generous grants are available for such conversions since by this means extra accommodation is made available at much less cost than building new property. Should you consider this plan, discuss the possibilities with a builder or architect, and get details of grants which you might obtain from the local Council. Sometimes a Council will be prepared to purchase your house and convert it into flats, allowing you to remain in one of them as a tenant.

If you rent a council house which is too large for you in retirement, you may well be able to change over to a smaller one or a flat, so releasing the other house for a family. Most councils are only too ready to co-operate in such cases since it means that their housing is being used to maximum advantage.

Those who retire from service accommodation, which they must vacate, face the most difficult prolems over their new homes. Unless they have capital to buy a property, or at least to put down a deposit and obtain a mortgage, they will need to find rented accommodation which is often very difficult. It is worth investigating the possibilities of help from one of the Housing Societies which now exist. They are set up to provide housing either by converting old houses into separate units or building new units especially for the purpose. The National Federation of Housing Societies will give the addresses of those societies in the area in which you are interested.

Assuming that you will be making a move to another home, what is it to be?

House, bungalow, flat or caravan?

To some extent this will be determined by what is available where and when you want it and there may be a wide choice or a narrow one, depending chiefly on the amount of money you have to spend and any special requirements you have. If you want to rent a property, then your choice is likely to be much more restricted. But you will doubtless start off with one or other of these possibilities as your first choice.

For some it will have to be a house with upstairs bedrooms, for, having slept all their lives above the ground floor, they could never be happy in a bungalow, or even a ground floor flat. To such it must be pointed out that stairs can be both difficult and dangerous in old age, and that a bungalow has much to commend it, besides removing this particular hazard. Maintenance is much easier and the handyman can, if he is so inclined, do most of the outside repairs and decorations himself. A further advantage, as I found by personal experience, is that most bungalows have ample roof space which, with the aid of a loft ladder, can be put to good use for storage.

The chief disadvantage of a bungalow is that it is more expensive to build than a two-storey house having the same accommodation and it occupies more ground space. The demand for bungalows is usually greater than for houses, especially in retirement areas, and this further enhances the price.

Many find that a flat suits them admirably since it involves a minimum amount of responsibility for outside house and garden maintenance. Provided there is a lift, the problem of stairs does not arise unless the lift breaks down! – and many seaside flats have wonderful views from their windows. The question of noise and neighbours, if you live in a flat, has to be taken into account and there can be difficulties if you have always been used to a house of your own.

The modern caravan has come a long way from the gypsy van that trundled along our roads. The modern residential type can be quite luxurious and, in relation to a house, quite cheap. Some who have been used to a touring caravan and who are able to keep their possessions to a minimum may find that a well-fitted caravan, on a pleasant site on which mains services are provided, can be quite successful as their retirement home.

Having decided on the type of home you want, what are the other factors you need to consider in looking for your new home, whether it is in the same district or somewhere else? The same factors as were considered under 'Where?' apply also under 'What?'

Family and Friends

I have already made the point that these are an important part of life, not least in retirement, so the choice of home must take account of this. Whether you are married or single, there are times when you will want to entertain people. A one-room flat may be convenient for all normal purposes but it does not give much scope for visitors.

The problem is to strike a compromise between what is needed for normal living and what is required to accommodate visitors. It is foolish to get a house which is large enough to take the maximum number of visitors you are likely to have, unless you plan to run it as a guest house. Running a large house and garden, if you have been used to it before, may be no problem when you have more time to give to it, but you need to look further ahead than the early years of retirement. My wife's parents bought a large house on retirement and as a family we enjoyed holidays with them for some years. But the time came when the garden became a burden and the house was much too large to look after, so they had to make a move to a flat when they were really too old for it. We took note of this in choosing our retirement bungalow which has only two bedrooms and a garden of modest size. There was a built-in garage which easily converted into an extra room, serving as dining-room/study and occasional bedroom. This gives us the extra space we need and with folding beds and bunks, we can put up a family with three children. It is worth having a slight squeeze for short periods rather than having to run a large house all the year round. Also it is essential that the place should not be too unwieldy for one partner to manage alone if and when that time comes. It is surprising what can be done in even a small home to accommodate temporary visitors.

So there is no need for anyone to feel lonely so long as they can maintain a guest room that is always available, and a meal table where there is always space for an extra seat. Mind you, some people value their peace and quiet. We bought our bungalow from an elderly couple who told us that on Bank Holidays they kept their telephone off the hook lest anyone should ring up and want to call on them. We were shattered at such an isolationist attitude!

Facilities

I have already dealt with the size of house in the

previous section but what about other features, such as the garden? The keen gardener will want a garden at least as large as the one he has been used to now that he will be able to give more time to it. But beware! A large garden can easily become a burden in a few years, and it is better to start with one of modest size, which you can supplement perhaps with an allotment so long as you are able to cultivate it. More books have been written about gardening than almost any other subject so there is little more here that needs to be said.

There are certain features of the house itself that are relevant to those who are growing older and, in retirement, we must face this fact of life. Heating is an increasingly important factor, both for comfort and health in old age. The relative advantages of electricity, gas, oil and solid fuel for central heating have been much debated, and each has its pros and cons.

Solid fuel is probably the cheapest of all but it involves much more work and mess than the others and on this account I would not recommend it. Gas is cheaper than either electricity or oil and is deservedly popular. Oil is convenient and clean, but the uncertainty over the price, and sometimes over the supply, is a disadvantage. Electric heating is the most expensive even when the cheaper rates for off peak supply to storage heaters are used, but it has much to commend it in spite of this. The installation is cheaper initially and requires virtually no maintenance such as is essential with the other forms of central heating. It is free also from the hazards associated with the use of gas for other purposes, such as cooking, which can be quite serious in the case of very old people, who may be forgetful.

In connection with heating of houses, much attention is being paid to the subject of insulation both in terms of cost and conservation. The lagging of the hot water cistern, whatever form of heating is used, is always well worth while. Adequate loft insulation not only makes for comfort but reduces the fuel bill. Double glazing is rather a luxury and, unless the window space is very great, it is doubtful whether cost can be recouped by fuel cost savings. The same must be said of cavity wall insulation which makes for a home with a more equable temperature but is not always economically justifiable. Overall carpeting helps to cut down heat loss through the floors and has the added advantage of greater safety. Polished floors may be attractive to look at but they constitute a serious danger to those who may not be too sure on their feet. Loose mats on a polished floor are a menace to old folk. The modern method of carpeting with squares is excellent as they are capable of being moved around to equalize wear.

The provision of adequate electric sockets around the house is something to look out for and, if rewiring is needed, the number and positioning of these sockets should be studied carefully. If possible, they should be located at waist level where they can be reached easily without having to bend down to the floor. Trailing leads should be avoided as they constitute a further hazard.

The kitchen is one of the most important rooms in the house. It should be well-lit both by natural and artificial light especially at the sink and over the working surfaces. These should be at the most convenient height to suit the person using them and the cost of moving them up or down an inch or so may well be worth while for the greater comfort of working at them. Avoid high shelves which call for the use of steps or a chair to reach them. Many home accidents occur due to elderly people trying to reach rather inaccessible storage places. It is a great advantage to have a house with ample, easily-reached storage space throughout.

On the subject of storage, what about a deep freeze? Maybe, like so many others these days, you have already proved how useful it can be and need no persuading. It was some years before we made up our minds to install one and we would not want to be without it now that we know its advantages. It stores any surplus fruit or vegetables from the garden, and it saves many a journey to the shops when one can go to it for meat and other supplies. With frequent visitors it is a boon, especially when they turn up unexpectedly, and one is never at a loss for a quick meal. It may not save money, but it saves work and time and worry all the year round.

For the handyman, workshop facilities are essential, so the size of the garage is important. If it is only just large enough for your car, assuming you have one, then you will need a shed or work room where you can keep your tools and do your jobs. If you manage without a car and still have a garage then you are fortunate indeed!

So far we have been considering only the case of retirement to your own home, wherever and whatever that may be, and whether it belongs to you or is rented. There are two other possibilities that call for brief comment.

Sheltered housing

There is little doubt that the majority of people who retire prefer to live as members of a normal community which includes young and old. They like to have the independence of their own home, and the freedom to find their own friends and follow their own pursuits without being made to feel different from those around them. To such folk, the idea of sheltered housing does not appeal; it sounds too much like segregation whereby the elderly are being kept away from other members of the community. But the term is a very broad one and covers many excellent schemes which, in the main, have been designed to help those senior citizens who by reason of advanced age or disabilities, or for other such reasons, need to live in a community which is specially geared to help them. There is a great variety of such schemes in many countries, particularly in the USA and Australia. Some have been sponsored by charities, churches and private groups. They usually comprise a complete housing estate, which is sometimes almost a small township in itself, with accommodation in bungalows or small units of various sizes, to suit different needs. A common feature is the provision of a resident warden or qualified nurse who can be called upon to give assistance in the day-to-day problems of residents, as well as being at hand for any emergency. The residents can usually enjoy independence to the degree that they wish, with all the facilities of a normal residence, but, in addition, can use certain communal facilities such as a central dining room and a recreation room. Some have their own shops and can cater for most of the residents' needs without their having to go far from their homes.

In this country, some similar retirement home estates have been set up by churches and by some professional institutions for their own members and they serve a very useful purpose. In some cases, it is necessary to take out a lease on the property, but others have a simple renting arrangement. One of the national organizations in this field is the Abbeyfield Society which sponsors numerous local housing societies which set up non-institutionalized family homes for groups of elderly people.

Some local councils have included similar schemes in their housing plans and groups of old people's bungalows or blocks of flats have been built. Sheltered housing may well appeal to those who prefer to be with others of their own age and who do not want to be bothered with house maintenance or gardening, especially if they suffer from some physical or other disability. It is not as yet generally available, and it should perhaps be looked upon as a possibility for a second move after retirement should it ever become necessary.

Residential accommodation

This is something we naturally associate with the very old, and as a stage well beyond the home to which we retire. It is natural for most of us to want to be independent and to live in our own homes just as long as it is possible. But the time may come to any of us when we can no longer do this, particularly if we are living on our own, and we shall need to move somewhere so that we can be looked after. This can mean either going to live with a relative, which is not always possible or even desirable, or going into some type of residential home. There are many of these run by local councils, others by charities or by private individuals, but the need is such that there are never enough. We may hope that the problem never arises for us personally, but the possibility is something to consider when deciding where to settle in retirement. It would be comforting to know that facilities do exist in your area and that, if the need arose, there would be somewhere to go.

Before we leave this subject of housing for retirement, I would again urge you to start thinking about the 'where' and 'what' of your retirement home in good time. To have settled on the area and to know what you are looking for, is more than half the battle when you start to look in earnest for the house of your dreams.

5
ANOTHER JOB?

Blessed is he who has found his work; and let him ask no further blessedness. (Thomas Carlyle)

If someone, who was about to retire, asked me, 'Shall I go on working?' I would answer most emphatically 'Of course you should!' It is absurd for those who come to the age of retirement to think that their working life has ended. In prospect, a life of leisure with no work to do may be pleasant and exciting; in practice, leisure time which requires a constant effort to fill it up becomes wearisome and frustrating. Anyone who has been unemployed will know that, quite apart from the financial problems involved, there is nothing more soul-destroying than to have to spend the day in idleness. The words of Thomas Carlyle, quoted above, are as true today as when he wrote them two hundred years ago.

So that is why I would urge most strongly that, so long as it is physically possible, everyone should go on working whatever their age may be. The dictionary defines working as being engaged in bodily or mental activity, and if being alive did not mean just this, we would be no better than cabbages!

The question that then arises, in relation to those who have retired from their jobs, is whether the work they will continue to do should be paid or unpaid. There will be some who will find in the normal activities of their own homes sufficient to occupy them all their time and, as the years pass, this is more and more likely to be the case. But few who have been working full time at their jobs up to retirement age will be satisfied merely to attend to their own home and garden and do nothing more just because they have reached 60 or 65.

There will be those whose circumstances are such that they have to go on with some sort of paid job in order to supplement their pensions. There are still many who do not qualify for an occupational pension and it will be some years before the new earnings related pension scheme does much to improve this situation. There are supplementary allowances available for those whose incomes fall below the minimum level, but not every pensioner will want to depend on this. Provided they can get some suitable work, many would prefer to be independent of such help, even though they are fully entitled to claim it.

Some will continue with their jobs because their skill and experience are still needed by their employers so it is mutually beneficial to continue working. Others will want to continue with a job not so much because they need the extra money but for the opportunity of meeting other people and the satisfaction it gives them of making their contribution to society. This applies specially to those who live on their own with all that can mean of loneliness and isolation. There are many who will find that they can get the satisfaction and fulfilment they need by engaging in voluntary work where the question of payment, other than possibly for out-of-pocket expenses, does not arise. This matter is dealt with in the next chapter.

Meanwhile, let us concentrate on the problems associated with finding a paid job after retirement. The pension position relative to those who have retired but continue working either full or part-time is dealt with later in Chapter 9, so it is not necessary to go into it here. The point that needs to be stressed is that in certain countries there are earnings rules in operation. In England this applies to men between the ages of 65 and 70 and women between 60 and 65 who are taking the N.R. Pension. During this period, if earnings exceed a maximum figure, which is adjusted from year to year, then there is a proportionate reduction in the pension. This limiting figure must be kept in mind when considering taking on another job.

What sort of job do you want?

Having decided that you want to get another paid job, then you need to make up your mind what sort of work you would like to do. Is it to be a part-time or full-time job? Do you want it primarily for the money or for the companionship? Do you want a manual or a clerical job? Indoors or outdoors? Do you like working with people or would you prefer to work on your own? Do you want to work for someone else, or would you like to be self-employed? You should ask yourself such questions as you start looking around for that new job. And it is well to start asking and looking well before you retire so that this becomes part of your pre-retirement planning.

Much will depend on your abilities and inclinations. You may have acquired special skills that you would like to be able to continue to use so that a job in the same field would suit you best. Or you may ask for nothing more than a quiet, easy job that will occupy your spare time usefully and profitably. On the other hand you may want a complete change and decide to launch out on a new career possibly in connection with some hobby or interest far removed from your previous work.

As you consider the matter, there are some general points to bear in mind. You will not be looking for a career that is to last you for a lifetime but for one that can at best be for a temporary period of a few years only. So it must be a job that brings you enjoyment as well as money and you must be able to do it without it ever becoming a strain or a burden. If it is a full-time job then remember that the longer you continue with it the less time you will have to enjoy being your own master, able to plan your own purposeful activity for each day.

Avoid any job that entails much travelling. You may have been used to commuting to work, but your retirement job should be as close to your home as possible to avoid the discomfort and cost of a long journey. Never be persuaded to put a lot of capital into a project such as a shop or small business which could involve you in much hard labour and long hours. Such a proposition might suit someone who has retired very early and can look forward to a further lengthy period of active life but it is not the job to take on at 65. Unless you are experienced in the running of a small business, with all the keeping of records and filling in of forms that is now involved, you are well advised to keep clear of it if you are a pensioner.

What can you offer?

You may have a very clear idea of the sort of job you want but you need also to know just what you have to offer to a prospective employer. Make a list of your qualifications and abilities so that you can judge what sort of job you could best tackle. Be frank with yourself and list your weak points as well as your strong ones! Some will have professional qualifications backed up by a lifetime's experience which could continue to be of great value in some fields. For example, an accountant can usually carry on in his profession well after retirement age, adjusting the amount of work to suit himself. The same applies to a woman who is a skilled dress-maker who need never lack work. On the other hand, those with the more specialized technical skills may find it more difficult to carry on for long in their particular line due to the very rapid rate of development in much modern technology. It is only those who are very closely involved in such work who can hope to keep pace with it.

So you must be realistic about your possibilities, and especially if you have held any sort of senior post, you will have to accept that retirement will mean a drop in status. That is why it is usually difficult for such a person to carry on working for a large organization after retirement, and for the sake of all concerned it is usually better to make a complete break and a fresh start.

Those who have been engaged in manual work, however skilled, are likely to find it more difficult to use their special abilities in retirement. At a time when there is much unemployment, there are many younger workers looking for jobs and there will not be many opportunities for pensioners to take up their old trade. So it means that they will have to look to something quite different from what they have been doing previously, though they might possibly be able to use the same skills in a different way.

You need to consider also what you can offer in the way of time. How many hours a day do you want to spend on the job? How many days, and what days do you think you can work? Some part-time jobs involve week-end and late night working. Are you prepared for this?

You should take into account your health. Maybe you are very fit and can still do a long hard day's work, but do you want, or do you need, to use the whole of your retirement time in this way when there must be many other things you would like to be able to do? Take into account the physical effort required for the job. Serving in a shop may seem an easy and pleasant way of earning some extra money, but that part-time shop assistant's job many have snags to it. It may mean being there just for the rush hours and this could prove very tiring if you have to stand all the time. Perhaps a sitting down job would be better for you and your legs!

What sort of work is available?

Much will depend on the locality and there is likely to be more scope in a country town than in a large industrial area where many of the workers remain after retirement. Clerical jobs are more likely to be available than manual ones. Part time and seasonal help is often needed by hotels, restaurants, clubs and shops, especially in the holiday areas. There are jobs in schools for helpers with school meals and as playtime supervisors, and school crossing patrols offer possibilities for both men and women. There is always a great need of women prepared to serve as home helps. They do wonderful service amongst the housebound and the elderly who live alone. This is a paid job but it is a real service to needy folk and can give great job satisfaction. The normal retirement age is 60 but you can serve on the reserve list up to 65.

In a number of places, occupation centres have been set up to provide work for retired men and women. They are known variously as Workshops for the Elderly, Sheltered Workshops and Work Centres for Retired People, and, as the need for them is becoming more widely recognized, their number is growing. Pioneering work in this field was done by the Rubery Owen organization in Darlaston where, as long ago as 1949, a Sons of Rest workshop was set up to which men from the factory, who wished to continue working after retirement, could be transferred. It operated on a 20-hour week, with morning and afternoon shifts, and work for the main factory was carried out by both skilled and unskilled labour. The idea has not caught on very well amongst other companies but similar workshops have been set up both by voluntary organizations and some local authorities. They cater for the retired of both sexes, although women seem to predominate, and they offer facilities for part-time work to suit individual needs. Their aim is to combine companionship, which for many is the most important feature, with useful occupation and paid employment.

The Employment Fellowship is an organization which encourages the setting up of such schemes and which co-ordinates their work. To quote from a recent report, they are using their experience in this field 'to make a direct contribution to the well-being and fulness of life for the large numbers of retired and elderly people who helped to lay the foundations of today's affluent society'.

There are many organizations, missionary societies, trusts and similar charities, which need to employ paid staff, often on a part-time basis. Such jobs are usually interesting and rewarding in the best sense even though financial stringency may limit the salaries that they can afford to pay. This is another field worth investigating.

So much for jobs that involve going out to work. What about work that can be done using your own home as the work place or base from which you operate? You can do this either by working for some organization or for yourself. You can work as an agent on commission for an insurance company, a travel organization, or a manufacturer, selling on the doorstep, or, as is sometimes done, by telephone. For such jobs you need to have some knowledge of selling and possess a pleasant manner as it means dealing with people all the time. Make sure that whatever you sell, whether services or goods, comes from a reputable source and has adequate back-up if anything should go wrong. This is a field which needs to be approached with great care as there have been unfortunate cases of dubious companies which have misled people by extravagant promises of profits and who have often required substantial down payments for goods which have never arrived. The law now offers some protection against swindles of this kind. However, they still happen and you need to be very cautious of any get-rich-quick proposition which is put to you.

Then there is work that you can do at home and which is entirely under your own control. The possibilities here are unlimited: the ex-typist, with a typewriter and duplicator, can start her own typing agency; the gardener, with more space than he needs himself, can raise plants and grow fruit and sell his produce; the carpenter or handyman can take on repair work; a husband and wife team, if their home is suitable and strategically placed, can set up to provide bed and breakfast accommodation. The experience of a lifetime can often be put to very good use in ways in which you are your own boss and can undertake as much work, or as little as you wish. There are craftsmen and craftswomen who can continue to use their skills so long as arm and eye permit – the watch or clock repairer, the dressmaker or knitter, the furniture repairer – these are just a few.

In the field of the arts there is scope too: the photographer, the artist, the engraver, and anyone with artistic ability and training can use his skills. In the world of literature, age is no bar to writing and some of the best books have been written well after retirement age. There is a market for articles and short stories in the numerous magazines that are published and even for whole books for those who have something to say and can say it well. Who would have thought that James Herriot's books about his life as a vet would have proved to be such an outstanding success?

Local papers often have work for an area reporter and for those who can write on specialist subjects such as local history or industry. Some hobbies can be made to bring in extra income: the stamp or coin collector who buys and sells as well as building up his collection; and the collector of antiques who haunts the salerooms and looks for bargains that he can sell again.

I have touched on only a few of the avenues that can be explored by those who wonder what sort of work is available for them. There surely is something you can find if you really try!

How can you find that job?

Knowing the sort of job you want and what you have to offer, how do you set about finding it? The obvious first move is to consult your local Job Centre where you will find displayed a list of job vacancies in your area. Some of these may be for part-time or specialist jobs for which you could offer your services. But even if nothing suitable is displayed, you can still talk to one of the staff about the possibilities of finding something to suit your need.

If nothing is forthcoming from the Job Centre, then you may find something in the advertisement columns of the local paper. Alternatively, if you feel that you are in a position to offer your services in a way that might be attractive to a prospective employer, then why not try putting your own advertisement in the paper? Set out to sell yourself! Make enquiries amongst your friends and acquaintances for possible openings and keep a look-out for developments in your area which might mean a job for you. It could be worth making a personal approach to local employers offering your skill in the hope that they might find something suitable. At a time when there is widespread unemployment, full-time jobs are not easy to come by but the demand for part-time labour is not affected to quite the same extent as the rest of the labour market; so do not be too discouraged if your first efforts are not successful. Persistence will usually find a way!

Apart from the locally advertised openings with which you are primarily concerned, there are certain central agencies which concentrate on finding work for those who have retired. The Employment Fellowship, previously mentioned, will be able to advise you about jobs in general and would put you in touch with one of the specialist agencies who might be able to help you. This would apply more particularly to those with professional qualifications or to specialists who might be prepared to consider jobs other than those close to their homes. The question of jobs overseas is dealt with in the next chapter where the emphasis is on voluntary work and where expenses only rather than a full salary are likely to be paid.

Statistics show that about half those who reach the statutory retirement age, both men and women, continue in a paid job, either full- or part-time, for a further four years. So it is clear from this that jobs do exist and that whoever you are there is a fair chance that you will be able to get one.

Although the subject of income tax, as it affects earnings after retirement, is dealt with in Chapter 9, it needs to be emphasized here that *all* other earnings have to be reported on your tax return form. This applies to income from any work such as we have been considering and to anyone regardless of age. If you work for yourself, it will probably be worth employing an accountant to help with your tax return form, as he will be aware of the allowances he can claim for you to cover necessary expenses associated with the job.

6
SERVICE FOR OTHERS

Let love make you serve one another. (Galatians 5:13)

Service is an overworked word which is used in so many connections that its basic meaning tends to be forgotten: we have to put up with an ever-growing Civil Service; we have the Armed Services and the Fire Service; and we call on the Social Services and the Health Service for a variety of aids to keep us alive. Most of these services are ours only because we pay for them in one way or another. Yet, in addition to all these services, there is an area of need that can only be met by what we call personal service which is the person-to-person help that no government-sponsored service can hope to supply.

It is in this area that unlimited opportunities exist whereby the retired person can give service for others; and it is an area in which the experience of a lifetime can be used to best advantage in helping other people. It is, of course, not at all necessary to wait for retirement to engage in some sort of service whether voluntary or otherwise. There are many who give the whole of their lives to such work. I refer to doctors, nurses, clergy, social workers and many others whose work is primarily concerned with human needs of one kind or another. There are, in addition, innumerable men and women who, in the midst of busy lives, still find time and energy for voluntary work in various fields of service. Because of their daily duties, whether in factory, office, shop or home, there is a limit to the time they can give to this work and so, on retirement, there is scope for extending both the amount of time and the range of such work that they can undertake.

For those who are already engaged in such activities there is likely to be little difficulty in continuing with them after retirement; but for some, whose lives have been overcrowded with other duties, the problem may be to find how best to make a start in voluntary work. So I want to make some suggestions as to various ways of tackling this problem in the hope that it will encourage greater participation in what is one of the most rewarding occupations, not in terms of money but in real job satisfaction. Only those who have engaged in it can appreciate what it means. I am sad when I sometimes see a couple settling down in retirement determined to keep themselves to themselves, with a stern resolve to confine their activities and interests to their home and garden, and to a small circle of family and friends. They want to avoid getting too involved with their neighbours. Nothing could be better calculated to bring on premature death from sheer boredom!

I suggest that the best way of looking at this subject is to consider it in terms of a series of concentric circles of influence and opportunity. We are each at the centre point of our circles, the smallest being that of our own family. As the circles expand to bring in other people so they take in first the local community, then the nation and finally the whole world, remote as that may seem to most of us. We may feel ourselves to be very small pebbles on the beach, but even one little stone dropped into a pool will send out ripples in ever-widening circles which eventually reach the very edges. So let us think about the possibilities of service for others within three major circles like this.

In the family of the Church

Let us begin with the extended family that one finds, or should find, in the fellowship of any church. I would stress that serving others in the context of the Church is only the starting point since, inherent in the membership of a Christian church, there should be a reaching out to others wherever and whenever there is human need. This is the principle laid down in the New Testament and this was the practice of the Early Church. Down the years, Christians have been foremost in the establishment of schools, hospitals and orphanages, to mention only a few of the ways in which they have responded to human need. It is only in recent years that the State has taken over much of this work and the Church's immediate involvement in these particular areas has greatly diminished. But in no way has the responsibility of the Christian lessened; human need has, if anything, increased and the opportunities of helping are much greater today than ever before.

It is unfortunate that the word *parochial* has come to be associated with a narrow-minded and limited outlook which sees the work of the Church as beginning and ending at the door to the church premises. Nothing could be further from the truth for the Church has been commissioned to serve not just its own members but the whole world. A church which fails to play its part in the life of the community and to reach out into the world at large, both as a corporate unit and through its individual members, is failing in its appointed task. The command given to the disciples was 'Go ye into all the world.' I believe that the Church should be the centre from which should flow service for others in those ever widening circles that reach out to the ends of the earth. It was John Wesley, that indefatigable servant of God, who affirmed: 'The world is my parish'.

Involvement in Christian work had an important bearing on our choice of a retirement home, for we made quite sure that we would be within reach of a church where we could be happy and useful. As it happened there was a choice of several in our district but there was one in particular where my services as a Reader were warmly welcomed and that decided us. Then, within a short time of moving to our new home, I was invited to take on the job of Deanery Treasurer, a job which at once involved me in deanery and diocesan responsibilities. So I was immediately put to work, nor has there been any let-up during subsequent years. My tasks for the church where we worship have ranged from taking the services to repairing the tower clock.

There are few churches which do not welcome new members, especially if they are prepared to put their shoulders to the wheel. Abilities of any kind can usually be put to good use. It may require special skill to do the flower arrangement but there are few who could not give a hand with the cleaning or with some of the other mundane jobs that are associated with the running of a church. What is most appreciated is a willingness to help with any job that needs to be done. Not everyone is called to the ministry of preaching or teaching, but help is usually needed in other ways such as the handling of the funds, the editing and distribution of the magazine and numerous such jobs.

Why are there so many faithful church members who are content to attend the services but who will not allow themselves to get involved more deeply? The result is that too much has to be done by too few and these are in danger of feeling themselves to be indispensable! This is bad for all concerned for, in the Christian family, everyone should be encouraged to take some share of the work. The quality which is sometimes termed stickability is most important, for the work can often be difficult and disappointing and the temptation comes to give it up, particularly if criticism is encountered. The one who earns respect is the one who takes on a job and keeps at it through thick and thin. The well-known hymn puts it rather well:

> Go, labour on; spend and be spent,
>   Thy joy to do the Father's will;
> It is the way the Master went;
>   Should not the servant tread it still?

A word of warning is needed here. Never carry on with a job beyond the point where you ought to give it up. Remember, the time must come when you should hand over to someone younger and it is better to recognize this yourself rather than to be asked to resign. Never hesitate to take on a job you know you can do well, even though you have grey hairs, or none at all! But, on the other hand, do give it up the moment you realize (or your wife has to tell you!) that it is time to pass it on to someone who will do it better.

There is a field of service in the Anglican Church through the Auxiliary Pastoral Ministry Scheme for older men who feel a call to the ordained ministry, whether they are still working or retired. They are referred to as supplementary, or non-stipendiary clergy, terms which are not very satisfactory but which are being used for want of a better designation. A special 3-year, non-residential course of studies, has to be undertaken and those who are ordained to this ministry are then fully qualified to officiate at communion and other services. Such men can give valuable help in the Church's ministry at a time when there is a growing shortage of full-time salaried clergy. For others, who wish to help with the services but who do not want to be ordained, there is open the office of Reader.

At one time, pastoral care in a parish was looked upon as very much the preserve of the minister and there are still some parishoners who are not satisfied with anything less than a visit from the vicar himself. But today, when an incumbent may have the care of several churches, it is not possible for him personally to cover the whole parish and he needs to delegate some of the work to suitable members of his congregation. Many churches have a system of road wardens whose task it is to keep an eye on members of the church in their area and to look out for newcomers so as to give them a welcome. This is a most useful field of service for anyone who has retired and can give the time to visiting the sick and the housebound and generally exercising pastoral care over a small sector of the parish.

The place of women in the Church, with special reference to the ordained ministry, is a subject of lively debate and in a number of churches they already have equal opportunities with men to serve as ministers. Partly perhaps because of tradition, not many aspire to serve in this way but none can deny that women play a vital role in the work of the Church both at home and overseas. Many of the jobs already mentioned are open to both sexes and both men and women can excel at them. But there are tasks which have traditionally been considered the preserve of women. We will look at hospitality more fully in Chapter 8 but here we might mention the useful contribution to church life a woman can make by taking a share in entertaining. Pastoral care can be exercised not only by visiting others in their homes, but by inviting to a meal newcomers, lonely folk and others in need of friendship and understanding. Where better can this service be rendered than in the relaxed atmosphere of a happy home?

In the local community

The next circle is one that is close at hand and almost unlimited in scope – so much so that there will be many for whom this field will be more than wide enough to occupy them fully without their needing to reach out any further. Community care is a comprehensive term covering the work being done both by social workers of all types as well as by an army of volunteers. It begins in the simplest possible way when you help a neighbour. It may be a widow who needs your advice on a business matter, or who wants help in her garden, or with some small repair which you can tackle and save her the very high service charge that she might otherwise have to pay. It can be summed up in the one word neighbourliness. Some districts operate Good Neighbour schemes whereby the residents of an area band together for mutual help and support, with special attention being paid to the more elderly and housebound amongst them, and in this way they supplement the work of the Social Services in a more personal manner. There are too few such schemes in operation and there is room for many more. It only needs someone who is prepared to give the time and thought to starting one up – and keeping it going!

In Britain, the National Health Service has taken over much of the work that used to be carried out by volunteer agencies, but there still remains much that calls for the sort of help that only volunteers can give.

Nearly every hospital has its League of Friends or some similar organization which recruits outside help to supplement the work of the professional staff. My wife has been closely involved with the League of Friends at a large psychiatric hospital where, for several years after we retired, she served part time as a social worker. The League organizes visitors to the hospital to take on lonely patients, sending them birthday and Christmas cards, and generally befriending them. They also organize the annual hospital fete which is a happy occasion for patients and friends and a useful fund-raising effort. Using the money raised by this and other events, they have built a Friends' Centre which provides a meeting place for the patients and their visitors, serving light refreshment in the evenings and at weekends. It is staffed almost entirely by voluntary helpers and provides a service beyond anything that the hospital itself could supply. Hospitals can also use volunteers for their car service and for the ward trolley services.

The WRVS is well known for the various ways in which it serves the community and it is closely involved with the Meals on Wheels service which relies almost entirely on volunteers for delivering to the homes of housebound people. Not only does this provide good hot meals at a subsidized price to those who may be unable to cook for themselves but it brings to many lonely folk a breath of friendliness to brighten their days.

Many towns now have community centres and clubs which provide occupation and interest both for old people and for the mentally and physically handicapped. Although they may be sponsored by the local authority, they all depend a great deal on the support and help of the people of the area. There is always scope for anyone who is willing to serve on the committee, to help with fund-raising or to take some other part in running such a centre. Many of them have started up just because someone had the vision to note the need, and the energy to work and inspire others until the dream became a reality.

The above are just a few of the many aspects of community care in which there is room for involvement by anyone who really wants to help. However there are some areas in which rather more specialised help is needed. The Samaritans, which is a national organization that operates through its local branches, provides a telephone lifeline for those in distress, with special emphasis on would-be suicides. Then there is the Marriage Guidance Council which is increasingly being called upon to advise over marital problems. There are a number of telephone 'help' organizations, some operated by a group of churches, which offer counsel and aid to those in need. All these depend on volunteers who must be willing to undergo some training beforehand. This type of work demands particular gifts of understanding and sympathy so it is not for everyone; but those who are prepared to take it up find it infinitely rewarding.

Of a more general nature is the work of the Citizens Advice Bureau which is a national organization but which works through local branches. It provides a valuable community service and can advise on a host of matters. Indeed, it seems able to answer almost any question put to it! Most branches are only too ready to welcome new helpers prepared to take on regular duty shifts.

As distinct from community care, which is concerned chiefly with the health and welfare needs of people there is the area of public administration and organizations concerned with local affairs. These offer unlimited scope for anyone with public spirit and a desire to serve the community. Each local Council needs to have on it men and women of experience and understanding, who can show that they are more concerned with the needs of people rather than with political dogmas. If you are a newcomer to a town it may take some time before you can become sufficiently well know to gain a place on the local council, but anyone who shows an interest and concern in local affairs will soon gain respect and support. Not everyone will aspire to be a town councillor but it is a field in which more should be concerned, especially church members. All too often they have failed to see that there is need for the Christian voice to be heard more in local affairs.

Most districts have a host of local organizations such as horticultural societies, sports clubs, music societies, choirs and similar groups which attract those with kindred interests. There is sure to be one at least which caters for your particular hobby or interest. Their problem is usually to find people willing to take office as committee members and officials. For those who want to play a part in this way there is no better method of making friends in a new district and becoming involved in the life of the local community.

A limited but needy field of service is open to anyone living within reasonable distance of any penal establishment. I mention this because I live near a medium security prison and am one of a small group of authorised prison visitors who pay regular visits to the prison and maintain contact with some of the prisoners. Not every man in prison is a hardened criminal; only a minority would come under this category. Many of them are the waifs and strays of society, unable to cope with life: alcoholics, drop-outs, rejects, homeless and friendless individuals. They have broken the law and are paying the penalty, but all too often there is little incentive other than to go on doing wrong again and again. Prison visiting is demanding and often disappointing work but the visitor is perhaps the only friend the prisoner has, his only contact who is not one of the 'establishment'. Anyone interested in work of this kind should contact the prison chaplain who will usually be only too pleased to have genuine offers of help.

This by no means exhausts the possibilities that are open to us in the local community. It is not really a matter of asking what we can do but rather of knowing what to choose out of the mass of voluntary work waiting to be done. Anyone involved in the sort of jobs we have been thinking about can have no doubt about being needed, and to feel needed is one of the greatest joys in life.

In the world at large

Once we leave the limited circle of the local community and look out on a field so large that it encircles the earth we may well feel at a loss to know what to do. Even if, after engaging in some of the tasks close at hand, we feel we can give further time and energy to other good causes in the wider world, where do we start and finish?

Consider, first of all, some of the societies and organizations whose work is primarily within our own country even though in many cases they may be associated with similar movements overseas. Many of these are church-based and are concerned with Christian work in various fields. There are youth movements such as the Crusaders, the Covenanters, and many others. Some societies such as the Scripture Union and the Church Pastoral Aid Society operate in conjunction with the churches and also provide a literature service. There are numerous home missionary societies such as the London City Mission and others working in particular areas of need amongst drug addicts, alcoholics and drop-outs.

There are other societies such as the National

Society for Cancer Relief and the National Society for Mentally Handicapped Children, and many more which concern themselves with health problems of various kinds. Others such as SHELTER specialize in homelessness and its related problems. There are some such as Age Concern and Help the Aged which focus on the needs of old people. The NSPCC is concerned with child neglect, whilst special groups have been set up to deal with family problems such as battered wives. There are numerous societies such as the RSPCA which care for animals, and others which are concerned with the protection of the environment.

The list could continue almost indefinitely. In every case much of the work must necessarily be done by volunteer labour and most of their support comes from voluntary subscriptions. These are all worthy causes but as individuals we find that we can only give financial help to a limited number, whilst we have to be even more selective in our choice of those to whom we can devote more time and attention by active participation. It is a good thing for these charities that our tastes vary so widely!

There will be for some people other national causes which may claim their interest and help – political parties, pressure groups, protest movements. So we can choose our cause and play our part as we wish.

So much for the national scene. What about the international? That the need of the world at large is immense is obvious now that our TV screens can transport us in sight and sound to the scene of the latest disaster area anywhere in the world. For most of us the help that we can give in such cases is not the person-to-person aid we give to our next door neighbour but that which we can give by proxy through one of the general relief agencies such as the Red Cross, Oxfam, Christian Aid, TEAR Fund or one of the other special agencies such as Help the Aged or the Save the Children Fund. These and numerous other funds are all worthy of our support as they operate on our behalf and depend entirely on our gifts to keep going. Nor is it simply a question of putting our hands in our pockets, for volunteers are needed to organize fund raising efforts of all kinds. The Oxfam shops raise a great deal of money and various agencies sell native handicraft work and by so doing provide occupation and encourage self help for many native village groups. This all involves voluntary work which takes time and demands organizing skill such as a retired person with some business experience would be well able to provide.

The churches have been pioneers in overseas aid. Not only have they taken the Gospel to many lands but they have sent out doctors, nurses and teachers all over the world, and are continuing to do so today. There are many missionary societies operating in different areas and each church is likely to have certain of these which it supports. Normally it might be expected that the only way in which a person who has retired could play a part in overseas aid would be by helping on the home front. So it may seem strange to suggest that overseas service for the over 60s is one of the possibilities now open to those who have retired.

Life overseas is nothing like as hazardous as it used to be. Modern medicine and improved living conditions have made it as safe and pleasant in many places as in the industrialized west. And short term service is now as much in demand in developing countries as lifetime service used to be in the early days of foreign missions.

I was reminded of this several years ago when my wife and I were visiting Nigeria where our daughter and her husband, who is a doctor, were doing a two year spell of duty in one of their large hospitals. Whilst there we met a missionary doctor who was returning to a bush hospital in a remote part of the country where skilled labour of any kind was practically unobtainable. When he learned that I was handy with tools of all kinds, he begged me to go back with him for a few months to help with many electrical and other jobs that needed to be done on his station. This would then give him more time for his medical work. Unfortunately our plans were such that it was not possible to accept his invitation but I would love to have been able to do so.

Many retired people in good health and with experience and skill in specialist fields such as medicine, accountancy, engineering, farming and such like could give valuable help overseas on a short term basis of months, or even years. There is frequent need for help in the installation of a new piece of equipment, or in a building project, or to help fill a gap due to illness or absence on leave. Previous experience of travel or of life overseas is not essential and it is open to anyone to offer help of this kind. No great expense need be involved for the cost of travel and accommodation is usually met by the organization concerned so that living costs would probably prove to be less than at home and arrangements can be made for a pension to be paid overseas.

One of the most remarkable examples of such

service is that of Lt.–Col. S H Middleton-West, FRCS, who served for many years in the Indian Medical Service. On retirement, he joined the Bible Churchmen's Missionary Society as a medical missionary and worked amongst the hill tribes in Burma. He retired a second time but returned to Burma after the Second World War to help re-establish hospitals there and he made his final tour of duty to a remote part of the country when he was 84. Not many are able to live so active a life to such a ripe old age but he would surely have considered youngsters of 65 well able to follow his good example. Dr Albert Schweitzer was another example of service for others continued well beyond the normal retirement age. He began his work for world peace when he was 70 and travelled widely up to the age of 84. He died at 90 still actively caring for the patients at the hospital at Lambarene, Gabon which he had founded many years earlier.

These two were medical experts but other skills are also needed by many countries in the Third World today. The carpenter, electrician, builder, motor mechanic can each use his skill and experience to help train those who will carry on with the job when he has left; the typist can help with correspondence and in the copying of manuscripts; the clerk can keep the books; the nurse can always find opportunities to use her nursing skill. There are many who complain that in retirement there is no chance for them to use the experience of a lifetime. Here is a wonderful opportunity to do just that!

The British Voluntary Service Overseas, although chiefly known for the part it plays in helping young people to take on short term voluntary work in the developing countries does also cater for older workers, and there are other agencies which provide opportunities for all ages. INTERSERVICE is an interdenominational information service sponsored by the Evangelical Alliance and the Evangelical Missionary Alliance which keeps a current file of Christian service opportunities available all over the world. They cover both home and overseas needs and will put the enquirer in touch with the society or church with a particular requirement which his skill or ability might be able to meet. Opportunities also arise through contacts with particular missionary societies and TEAR Fund operates STOP (Short Term Overseas Personnel) through which they second workers to clearly defined jobs in areas of special need.

Another organization called Christians Abroad, which is supported by Christian Aid, the British Missionary Societies and the Ministry of Overseas Development, can advise regarding work opportunities in the overseas field for which, in many cases, a normal salary would be paid.

A short spell of service abroad could be an exciting and satisfying start to retirement. If you consider it then it would be wise to start planning in principle, if not in detail, well before you actually retire.

A word of warning

Try to avoid two extremes: the first is that of not doing as much for others as you could do and the second is of trying to do too much. The first shows a failure to recognize your potential and the second a failure to accept your limitations. For example, to take on a small job such as that of a sidesman who has to be on duty once or twice a month, or to accept membership of a committee that meets just a few times a year, and to feel satisfied with this as your 'service for others' might mean that you are not using your full potential. On the other hand, to take on more than you can cope with and to risk breakdown and worry because things get on top of you is foolish and counter-productive. The problem we all have is to find the right balance between too little and too much. Capability and capacity for work vary greatly from one individual to another and we each must determine our own limits, physical and mental, and keep to them. One of the hardest things to do is to learn to say 'No' when asked to take on just one more task! Perhaps if those who fail to do enough did more then those who try to do too much would be able to do less!

I feel that I have only touched the edge of this subject but perhaps I have written enough to indicate the tremendous scope there is in Service-for-Others. Whatever voluntary work you take on, you should find in it pleasure beyond anything you might get from a paid job. Furthermore, you can be happy in the knowledge that you are following in the footsteps of One who came, 'not to be served but to serve' and whose command we noted at the start of this chapter, 'Let love make you serve one another'.

7
HOBBIES AND INTERESTS

All work and no play makes Jack a dull boy. (Old proverb)

This well-known saying is true whether Jack is a young boy or an old one. We all need to have interests for our leisure hours which give us a change from our daily work. This is vital during our working lives and is also necessary when retirement brings us leisure days in place of hours. I have heard a wife remark about her husband, as retirement approaches, 'He hasn't any interests outside his job so I don't know how he is going to fill in his time. I don't want him sitting around all day reading and watching the telly.' How dull that would be for him, and for her too! Fortunately, most men have hobbies and interests that make them look forward to the time when they will be able to devote more attention to them. The golfer longs for the opportunity to enjoy his game any and every day so that he can avoid the overcrowding on the greens at the weekend. The gardener pictures his garden kept in apple-pie order when he is able to give all his time to it. But the golfer and the gardener have to ask themselves what they will do when the weather is too bad for them to follow their chief pursuits and how they will face those long winter evenings. It is a joke between my wife and myself that we are still looking for them!

Time on your hands

There are two words connected with this topic that I would like to mention. The first is 'pastime', a word which I dislike because of its implications. It seems to suggest that someone has time to spare and needs to find some way of using it up. Perhaps it might be applicable to the prisoner in a dungeon or the sailor marooned on a small boat! But it is not a word that should be relevant to most of us in normal circumstances. Perhaps I am being unduly critical of a word that is harmless in itself but I hope you see my point. There ought to be a purpose in everything we do including the way we spend our spare time. Aimlessness is all too common a feature of modern society and from it stems much of the violence and vandalism of today. Life should at all times have a purpose and the lack of it is to be deplored whether in the young or the old.

The other word is recreation and this by contrast should be relevant to any hobby or interest. I like to think of it in its basic meaning of re-creation. It is a word with a strong, positive ring about it. A recreation ground is a purposeful place offering to all ages the possibility of exercise and enjoyment in a variety of sports. So the idea of re-creation should have its place in any leisure activity in which we engage. It can apply to body, mind or spirit for each in turn needs constantly to be renewed.

Mr David Hobden, Director of Age Concern, commenting on the problems likely to arise from the reduction of working hours, the lowering of the age of retirement and the consequent increase in leisure time said that 'having too much time with too little to do could become for many a living hell.

People of all ages will be desperately searching for some role. Golf, bridge, whist or bingo, digging a garden, hours of television, will begin to pall. They are not in themselves enough on which to build a full life for the majority.'

Throughout this book, I have been trying to stress the need to cultivate a wide spectrum of interests and activities in order to live a full life. What would life be like if we saw everything as on the screen of a black and white TV set? Colour makes such a difference to our enjoyment of life and it is in the number and variety of our interests that life takes on its full meaning. So, as one way of tackling this subject, I suggest that you take stock of your own particular hobbies and interests in terms of their objectives. Ask yourself these various questions, about each of them.

Does it entertain?

The word entertainment was orginally associated with hospitality but it has come to have a much broader meaning and can now be applied, according to the dictionary, to 'any pleasurable performance'. We can be entertained by reading a book, by listening to music or a radio programme, or by viewing a play or performance of any kind whether live or on TV. The purpose of entertainment, whether it be light or serious, is to give us pleasure and to provide that which will take our minds off the difficulties and problems of daily life. It can be of great value in releasing some of the tensions that build up within us; it gives us the relaxation which we all need from time to time.

So, entertainment, which has a great variety of forms, rightly occupies a part of our leisure time; but it should be only a part. Therein lies the danger with television, an entertainment medium which is available in nearly every home for most of the hours of the day and which asks from us nothing more energetic than sitting and watching. It has been estimated that the average person today will spend the equivalent of 15 years of life viewing TV. What a terrifying prospect! Of course, it is a boon to those who, by reason of old age or infirmity, are unable to leave their homes since it can bring the world right into their rooms and relieve boredom. But for the able-bodied, it is a form of entertainment which should be used with discrimination, for it is a mixture of good and bad; and with restraint, for too much television can keep us from pursuits that are much more worthwhile.

An excess of passive entertainment, in which we only look and listen, will encourage lassitude; and the relaxation we legitimately seek can then degenerate into laziness of mind and body. Active participation in the field of entertainment can be as satisfying to the individual as to those being entertained. Membership of a choir or of an orchestra provides a pleasant occupation and congenial companionship during practices quite apart from the pleasure it gives to those who listen to the public performances, though here again we must be prepared to give up as our voice or skill deteriorates. Even the solitary exercise of reading a book for our own pleasure can become active entertainment for others as well if we read aloud on to a tape so that some blind person could enjoy it too.

Is it creative?

There will be a positive answer to this question in a great number of hobbies both for men and women. Handicraft skills come into play in a host of leisure activities from the knitting of socks to the making of furniture, from painting a portrait to decorating a house, from preparing an appetizing meal (some husbands make a hobby of this!) to flower arranging. There is always great satisfaction when we can look at something that our hands have made.

There will always be those who will say, 'But I'm no good with my hands,' and this is often an excuse rather than a reason for not trying. I do not believe there is anyone really incapable of finding a productive hobby of some kind. Many do not require either technical ability or the skilled use of tools. Not everyone aspires to work such as restoring antique furniture or repairing clocks but there are many simple but interesting things that can be made by anyone prepared to take time over it. Books without number are now available on handicraft work of all types and many evening institutes offer courses and provide expert tuition for the budding craftsman of any age.

One of the best examples of a creative hobby is gardening, though perhaps *productive* would be a better description of it. The gardener does not need to be an expert with green fingers to show that he can produce beautiful flowers and useful vegetables. He soon learns that this is a job where he is really only the assistant, however clever he may be. He may only recognize a vague force that he calls nature which does most of the work for him; or he may see, as many of us do, the hand of God, the Creator, in what grows out of the ground.

Creative work is seen in much more than the things that skilled hands can make. A poem, a play or a piece of music are the products of skilled minds. Man was 'made in the image of God' and surely this is reflected in the creative abilities latent in most people but so often never given a chance to be exercised. Today many work at repetitive jobs which are deadly dull so there is all the more need for spare time interests which will encourage the mind and hands to more creative effort. Retirement activities which can be of our own choosing should never be boring or uninteresting. If they are then it is time to take up something creative in which interest and fulfilment can be found.

Is it instructive?

It has been said that if we stop learning then we stop living. Education is a process which starts in the cradle and goes on to the grave. Many hobbies are by their very nature educational: the stamp collector must constantly keep abreast of new issues and developments in philately; the radio ham must study his subject so as to keep up with the latest technological advances; the naturalist and the bird watcher must always be extending their knowledge of their subjects. Indeed there must be few spare time interests which do not involve some study and consequent advance in knowledge. A great deal of the pleasure we get from a hobby is finding out more about it and applying that knowledge to it. There are magazines and books on hobbies and spare time pursuits of all kinds and your local library will generally be able to obtain a book on your particular subject however unusual it may be. It may even be possible to borrow a book on extended loan, should you need it for prolonged study. And if you know of some new book that is being published which you would like to read why not put in a suggestion that your library adds it to its shelves? Indeed your local library can play an important part in your retirement life. Make sure you know about its services.

Educational opportunities for those who have retired go far beyond the special courses for senior citizens that some local authorities run, which are well worth attending. Often there are other interesting courses open to all ages which you could take. During the first winter of my retirement I took a course on Small Boat Navigation and another on Appreciation of Antiques. Both were entirely new subjects to me but I found them interesting and stimulating. To tackle a new subject, such as learning a language, is a great challenge and a real mental stimulus. It is sometimes said that you can't teach old dogs new tricks but this is not true. You can, but it takes longer, and more time is just what should be available to those who have retired.

There are some who at 70+ have taken a degree and this is quite possible through the Open University courses. These can be followed up on TV and cover a wide range of subjects. Information about every form of adult education, including various residential short time courses, can be obtained from the National Institute of Adult Education or the Workers' Educational Association.

Further education, in a subject that appeals to you, can be an exciting, pleasant and profitable use of your time.

Is it good for your health?

In nearly every form of sport available for the over 60's, there is the primary benefit of improved physical fitness for, as far as is humanly possible, we all ought to indulge in some form of bodily exercise, even if it is nothing more strenuous than walking. Those who own a dog will know that the daily walks are both necessary for the dog and good for its owner. The gardener too can bear witness to the importance and value of exercise. Even if the results of his planting are disappointing, he knows that the physical effort that it has involved in the open air has been good for his health. Again though we should add the proviso that too much physical exercise can be bad and everyone should learn his own limitations.

Card games of all kinds help to keep the mind alert though the element of physical activity is lacking from them. The daily crossword puzzle, which many enjoy solving, is a useful way of flexing the mind but it is not the only way of ensuring that the reasoning faculties do not deteriorate. Mental health is quite as important as physical fitness and those hobbies which stimulate both mind and body should find a place on your list. The naturalist, the archaeologist, the fossil collector and many like them exercise their bodies and their minds in the pursuit of their hobbies. All the hobbies and interests with which we occupy our leisure time ought to help to keep us fit both physically and mentally.

Is it lucrative?

It is not usual to take up a hobby in order to make money. Indeed, it is more often the case that a good deal of money is spent in pursuit of our hobbies. So it may be necessary to consider whether the cost involved, which we might well have been able to afford before retirement, is justifiable and possible afterwards. We need, therefore, to look at the negative as well as the positive aspects of this question. It is pointless to continue with a hobby which is expensive beyond our means; any pleasure we might get out of it would be counterbalanced by the anxiety over what it was costing us.

But there are some hobbies that can be turned to good account financially and you may find that, with extra time available, you can use the skill or experience gained in the pursuit of some particular hobby to supplement your pension. If you do turn a spare time activity into a time-consuming and money-making business then it can take the place of the job you had before and you may then need to consider what quite different interests you will need to provide relaxation from it! If you have plenty of other interests already then this will be no problem.

Profitability, which is another aspect of this question, can be a useful part of many spare time pursuits without having to be considered as extra earnings. The produce of a garden may not bring in any actual cash but it does save money that would otherwise have to be spent on fruit and vegetables. Toys of all sorts such as teddy bears or dolls' houses produced as presents can represent quite substantial savings and grandparents, or kind aunts and uncles, who can exercise their skills in this way will never lack for happy and useful occupation. In these days when such items bought from the shops are very expensive, the handyman, or handywoman, who can buy good secondhand toys and remake them as new will find this a very profitable exercise.

To conclude

We could ask other questions such as whether our interests include both indoor and outdoor occupations. They certainly should do for we cannot always expect good weather. Also we should ask if some of our hobbies are pursued solo and some in company with other people. A right balance between the two is necessary.

So, having reviewed the situation as far as your own hobbies and interests are concerned, you will be better prepared to face the leisure days that retirement brings. I am sure there will be many who will answer positively all the questions except possibly the last. Whether hobbies are lucrative or not is, for most of us, not really important but the other questions are. If your interests are many and varied, then you should have no problems unless you find, as some of us do, that the days are too short! This may be a difficulty but it should never be a worry.

But I fear there will be some, like the husband I mentioned at the start of this chapter, who are desperately short of interests outside their jobs and who dread the empty hours ahead of them. How can they be helped?

Here are a few suggestions. There will usually be some interest, however slight, to work upon, some subject that arouses faint response. Take that as a starting point and build upon it, study it and develop it to the point where a passing interest becomes something really absorbing. Then move on to associated interests. For example, the person whose sole interest is in reading could expand that into collecting books about, or researching on, some particular subject, or a famous individual or event. From that the hobby could develop into writing or lecturing on that subject. Or interest in books could be directed into such practical skills as book binding or the repairing of old books.

Perhaps some, who are wondering how best to use their spare time, could look again at the suggestions made in the last chapter about service for others. It is an exhilarating and absorbing occupation to help those who are in need, whether it be the next door neighbours or the refugees on the other side of the world. Any of the relief organizations will be only too ready to make good use of time, energy or skill that is offered to them.

How you spend your spare time is something you alone can decide. No one can tell you what to do but if you are to enjoy doing it then it must be your own choice. Your problem may be to know what to choose from the bewildering range of possibilities open to you.

Before we leave this subject, there is one strong recommendation I would make to everyone. Try, as far as possible, to have in hand at any one time one major project. It should be something definite with a target date for completion. It might be the building of an extension to the house, or constructing a sun room, or a greenhouse. It could be the writing of a book on some subject in which you feel you can make a contribution that would be of interest to others. This book on retirement has been my major project for some time and during the final stages it has demanded priority over everything else. Your project could be the starting up of some club or society for which there is a need. Or it might be the making of a model that needs much time and concentration, or the development of an idea that you have of some novelty that might be patentable or at least of some interest to a manufacturer. It might be the organizing of some event; an exhibition, a fête or a conference. Soon after my retirement, I was asked to act as honorary organizer of a national conference on evangelism which turned out to be a two year task entailing a lot of work and travelling, all of which I very much enjoyed. So my advice from experience is that you should select a major task, enjoy doing it but keep your other interests going as well.

8
FRIENDSHIP AND HOSPITALITY

Hail Guest! We ask not what thou art;
If Friend, we greet thee, hand and heart;
If Stranger, such no longer be;
If Foe, our love shall conquer thee. (Old Welsh Door Verse, Arthur Guiterman)

Friendship is a two-way thing and has to be worked at. It cannot be bought with money yet it is more precious than any earthly wealth. As we grow older we find that our friends may become fewer but we value them so much the more. Shakespeare's advice still holds good:

'Those friends thou hast, and their adoption tried,
Grapple them to thy soul with hoops of steel'.

The question of friendship is one of the most important factors when contemplating a move to a new place after retirement and I have already touched on this aspect of it in connection with housing in Chapter 4. If friends of long standing are left behind and new ones are not quickly made to take their place, then the move can prove disastrous. The Englishman is noted for regarding his home as his castle and his wife may take the same view. So, when such a couple retire to a new area they may soon find themselves desperately lonely. It applies particularly in a village situation where newcomers who show that they feel themselves to be superior to the 'yokels' find themselves isolated from the life of the community. This can happen also in a town or large housing estate although it may be less noticeable there. The fault is usually with the newcomer who too often fails to realize that friendliness begets friendship. Unless the stranger makes the first move, or at least goes half way there for a start, he will be judged to be stuck-up and will be left alone. So if you claim you have no friends, stop and think. Whose fault is it really?

A friend of mine retired to a village where for several years beforehand he had had a holiday cottage. During previous holidays he had taken pains to get to know nearly everyone in the village and by the time he retired he was on Christian name terms with them. Immediately he became part of the village community, entering into its life, helping with the annual fête and all the other local events. He went out of his way to show himself friendly from the start and he now lives a full, interesting and satisfying life, being accepted almost as an old inhabitant!

When my wife and I moved down South on retirement, we wondered whether our remoteness from friends in other parts of the country would cut us off from them but it has proved otherwise. We have our friends locally but being at the seaside has acted as a magnet for many other friends who drop in to see us or come to stay.

As years increase and mobility decreases, so loneliness can become a real problem. It is inevitable that the circle of our friends will grow smaller in time and we must be prepared for this to happen and be willing to accept the fact. I well remember my father, having reached his century, saying, rather sadly, 'I've outlived every one of my contemporaries.' But the crowd of family and friends who gathered around him to celebrate his birthday showed that he still had many who loved and cared for him.

Loneliness depends less upon circumstances than upon the attitude of mind of the individual concerned. Some invalids are so outgoing in their attitudes that it is difficult to realize that they are confined to their rooms. Such people seldom lack visitors. There is no surer way of losing friends than by becoming so obsessed with our own problems, our aches and pains, that they become the sole topic of thought and conversation. Pre-occupation with self is a sure recipe for loneliness!

One problem with lonely folk is their reluctance to let their visitors go. They are so gratified to see them that they do not want to lose them. How often the remark is made, 'I dare not go to visit that person as I know I shall never be able to get away.' This desire of a lonely person to hang on to a visitor is natural and understandable but it is counter-productive. If it were possible to drop in for just a short chat, many more people would be willing to visit the lonely and the lonely ones would have more visits.

This emphasizes the need for more understanding and neighbourliness on the part of those of us who are fit and well and can engage in this form of ministry. Too often in the past this task has been looked upon as the preserve of the parson or the social worker. Yet it is a field of service where those who have retired can help to relieve the boredom and loneliness from which so many elderly people suffer. We should recall that the time may come when we may be confined to our room, or our bed, and when we in turn will be glad to welcome a friendly visitor.

The development of high-rise flats in recent years has done much to increase loneliness amongst the old for it has destroyed the 'over-the-fence' friendliness which characterized the little terraced houses of Victorian England. But wherever we live, in a little village or a large block of flats, there will usually be those not far away who are older than we are, or less mobile and more lonely, who would welcome a friendly approach and the occasional visit to relieve their boredom.

I have called this chapter 'Friendship and Hospitality' because the two are so closely associated. It was my wife's privilege and mine also to be brought up in homes which kept an open door for visitors. I recall many an occasion when as a boy I slept on a makeshift bed on the floor because the room that my brother and I occupied was given up to visitors. There was one whom I remember very vividly. He was a missionary from the West Indies, a patriarchal figure with a long white beard and he used to sit me on his knee when I was very small and tickle my face with the tip of his beard! My parents had only a small house and a small income but it was a happy home, rich in friendship and hospitality.

Why is it that in so many homes hospitality is limited to members of the family or to friends in return for, or in expectation of, their invitations? Homes that are open to anyone in need, and especially to those who are not in a position to offer any return hospitality are all too few. Hebrews 13:2 has an interesting comment on this subject,

'Remember to show hospitality. There are some who, by so doing, have entertained angels without knowing it!' And what better encouragement to hospitality could there be than that given by our Lord in Matthew 25:40 'I tell you this: anything you did for one of my brothers here, however humble, you did for me.'

There are those who would like to show hospitality but are nervous about inviting strangers into their homes lest they should fail to entertain them properly. They feel rather like the bather on the edge of the pool who hesitates to take the plunge, in case the water is cold. But those who do jump in find that the experience is most rewarding. The cost of hospitality is principally in time and thought but this is nothing compared with the pleasure it gives and the blessing it brings. Students are one group who especially welcome hospitality in homes as a pleasant change from their hostels or lodgings. Many are from overseas and have few contacts in their new country. There are other lonely and friendless folk in most places and it should not be too difficult to search them out. The need to foster friendship and understanding with those of other races is only too obvious in view of the tensions that exist in Britain today and meeting round a meal table is one of the best ways of getting to know such people. It is a first step on the road to racial harmony. In most cities there is a branch of the British Council and they are usually aware of the needs of those from other lands who would welcome an invitation to an English home. There is great need for such hospitality around Christmas and Easter and the Universities and Colleges Christian Fellowship operate a hospitality scheme and will gladly put potential hosts in touch with suitable students. Another national organization is Contact which maintains a register of those willing to take old and lonely folk out for an afternoon and to invite them back home for tea occasionally. There are numerous local associations which operate in much the same way.

Those who are church members should not find it difficult to discover others in their own congregation who would greatly benefit from friendship and hospitality. There are unlimited opportunities for those who are willing to show kindness to others less fortunate than themselves. The WRVS does splendid work in this field and would always be happy to have offers of help.

The Welfare State has done much to relieve the grinding poverty of previous years and the various cash benefits now available can help to pay fuel and grocers' bills but they cannot buy friendship. Money alone will not relieve loneliness but the love and care of those who will give themselves to help lonely people around them can do much to meet the need.

The latest moves by the psychiatric hospitals to put many of their less ill patients out into the community in small self-contained groups provide an excellent opportunity for other members of the community to share in the work of rehabilitation. The patients may seem repressed and inhibited but it is wonderful how they relax and open up like flowers in the sunshine when they encounter the friendly atmosphere of a stable home. There is a saying that 'where there's a will there's a way,' and this applies to all those prepared to share with others less fortunate than themselves some of the blessings of their own happy homes.

A more difficult and rather limited field is that of ex-prisoners who, if they are ever to be properly rehabilitated and restored to an honest way of life, need all the encouragement and help that can be given to them. In many parts of the world people are working on this problem. In New Zealand there are open prisons which are closely linked with the place where they are situated. The local community takes an active interest in the work of the prison and the prisoners themselves are allowed to spend Sundays and week ends in local homes where they are helped to readjust to normal family life before their release. Not all prisoners respond to this sort of treatment but there are many who have never known what it is to live in a happy home and for them it can prove to be a turning point.

So open your home if you can. You'll probably enjoy it and there will be amusing incidents to look back on. We often recall one guest who talked too much. The meal lasted for two hours and at times we wondered whether the food on his fork would ever reach his mouth!

I recall another occasion during the Second World War when we invited two soldiers in for a meal at Christmas time and we did our best with the limited rations to put on a good spread for them. My wife began to offer more food as soon as she saw an empty plate but one of them stopped her, saying, 'Don't you worry, Mam, we're going right round the table'. And they did!

9
MONEY MATTERS

Where your treasure is there will your heart be also.
(Matthew 6:21)

I have left this chapter on finance until nearly the end of the book quite deliberately. It is not that money is unimportant, but that there are other more important ingredients which make for a happy and successful retirement. Of course, an adequate income, even though it does not of itself bring happiness, does help. To face retirement in penury, as used to be the lot of so many not so long ago, is a wretched prospect that no one should have to look forward to.

What is an adequate income? This is, of course, a relative term. What would provide enough and to spare for one person would seem like abject poverty for another. So much depends on what we consider to be the standard of living that we should enjoy in our retirement and this is conditioned by what we had before. Our basic needs of food, clothing and shelter do not vary a great deal and are comparatively cheap, so long as the emphasis is on the word basic. It is those extras, the things that have come to be considered as essentials in the Western world, that cost so much. We think of the people of the Third World as being deprived when they lack the bare necessities of life but we consider ourselves approaching poverty if we do not have a car, a colour TV or a washing machine!

It has been my privilege to travel on business in various parts of Africa and India and, having seen how people live in those lands, it is not difficult for me to appreciate how fortunate we are in this country. To see poverty and destitution on the T.V. screen can never bring it home to us in the same way as a walk through the slums of, for example, the city of Calcutta. Anyone who is inclined to grumble at what some wrongly refer to as our falling standard of living might try this as a sure remedy!

Contrary to what so much modern advertising tries to tell us, the possession of things cannot bring happiness or contentment. This truth was emphasized by Christ when he said, 'Even when a man has more than enough, his wealth does not give him life.' (Luke 12:15) (N.E.B) Some of the happiest people I know have very few possessions and live on very limited incomes. Yet we know from our daily papers that some of the most unhappy often have more money than they know what to do with. The story is told of a man who called his retirement home Great Gain. This excited much speculation amongst his neighbours who wondered if he had won a fortune on the pools. When questioned, he used to quote a verse from 1 Timothy 6:6. 'Godliness with contentment is *great gain.*' Or, as the Living Bible puts it, 'Do you want to be truly rich? You already are if you are happy and good.' That man had learned the secret of contentment. So had the Apostle Paul who wrote (Philippians 4:12 Living Bible) 'I know how to live on almost nothing or with everything. I have learned the secret of contentment in every situation, whether it be a full stomach or hunger, plenty or want.'

I hope I have not laboured this point but I think we need to grasp this truth before starting to discuss what I would call the mechanics of finance. We ought to manage our money wisely and well and we shall do this best if we have the right attitude to it. It is the way we look at money rather than the amount of it that will determine the quality of our lives.

After I had read a number of books and articles by financial experts on the subject of retirement finance and began to appreciate the complexity of the subject, I almost gave up! It would have been so easy simply to have referred you to their weighty tomes and left it at that. However, I decided to go on and, with valuable help from experts, I have tried to outline what seems to me to be the important points that ought to be considered. It is obviously impossible within the compass of one chapter to deal with every aspect of retirement finance but I hope it will serve as a useful introduction to the subject and encourage you to go into it more deeply with the help of such books and experts as may be available to you. I shall be quoting very little in the way of actual figures for they are constantly changing and the only safe way is to get the up-to-date information from the latest Government leaflets or other applicable literature.

Your income

Most of us have to face the fact that our income will drop on retirement so one of the first tasks to tackle, well before the actual date, is to make a realistic assessment of your financial position, your expected income and your expenditure. For those who have been working, there will be the National Retirement Pension plus, for many of them, a pension from their employers. Then there may be other income from work which you or your wife may be doing after your retirement plus any investment income from money you may have saved. We will consider these items separately.

National insurance retirement pension

Provided you have made the necessary number of contributions to the National Insurance Scheme, you will receive the full N. R. Pension. About four months before you reach minimum retirement age (65 for men and 60 for women) you should receive an invitation to claim your pension. If you have any doubts about your pension position or are proposing to continue working and wish to defer your pension, then you should discuss it with the local office of the Department of Health and Social Security.

A pension book is provided when your pension has been awarded and this enables you to draw it weekly at your most convenient post office. Alternatively, it can be paid by warrant which you can pay into your bank account in four-weekly or quarterly amounts in arrears.

Here are a few supplementary points in connection with the N. R. Pension but for full details you should obtain the appropriate official leaflets.

A small addition to pension is paid to pensioners over 80.

A husband's pension will normally be increased by an allowance for his wife if she is living with him, regardless of her age. This allowance will not be paid until he had claimed his pension even though his wife by then may be over 60. However, if the wife has been working and paying her own contributions she can claim her own retirement pension at 60 on the basis of her own contributions.

The widow of a pensioner who has been receiving the lower married women's pension up to the time of his death will then be entitled to receive the larger single person's pension regardless of whether or not she has paid any contributions.

The basic retirement pension will continue to be protected against increases in prices or the level of earnings whichever is most beneficial to pensioners.

Working after retirement

There are various regulations which affect the person who continues working after reaching the minimum pension age and these can be considered briefly by taking some typical cases. These will only give a general guide and it would be wise to discuss your own particular case with the Pensions Department at the local office of the Department of Health and Social Security.

Working after early retirement

If a man or woman retires from a job, possibly with an occupational pension, they cannot claim the N. R. Pension until they reach the minimum retirement age. If they take on a paid job and earn above a stipulated minimum, or work for themselves, they must continue to pay Social Security contributions until they reach minimum pension age. During this time they will continue to be eligible to claim unemployment, sickness and invalidity benefits in the normal way.

Working after reaching minimum retirement age – pension deferred

Men or women can continue working normally after they reach this point and defer for a time claiming their N. R. Pension and when they eventually retire, or reach the age (70 for a man, 65 for a woman) when they will automatically be treated as retired, they will receive their pension at an increased rate depending on the period of deferment. No contributions have to be paid after reaching the minimum retirement age but those who defer taking their pensions can continue to claim unemployment, sickness and invalidity benefits during the deferment period. The rate of benefit will be restricted to the rate of retirement pension to which they would have been entitled had they actually retired.

Working after reaching minimum retirement age – pension claimed.

For those who continue to work after being awarded their retirement pension the earnings rule comes into operation and the pension is reduced on a sliding scale after a certain level of earnings has been exceeded. In assessing earnings, reasonable allowance is made for expenses incurred necessarily in connection with the employment such as travelling and meals. The stipulated level of earnings is adjusted from year to year to keep pace with average national earnings but you can assume that the whole of the pension will have been deducted by the time your earnings reach the national average. This means that for most pensioners there is good reason for limiting any earnings to the permitted level. If earnings are likely to exceed the stipulated level then it would pay to defer taking the pension for a period as mentioned above.

The earnings rule no longer applies after a man reaches the age of 70, or a woman the age of 65, when the N. R. Pension is paid in full regardless of the amount that is earned.

Employment income

As already pointed out, pensioners and their wives are able to continue working within certain limits without their pensions being affected and for some this may be a necessary method of supplementing their pension. For tax purposes, the total earnings and pension must be declared and it is the joint income of husband and wife that is normally assessed for tax. In certain cases, particularly when the wife is earning a substantial salary, it may be more favourable for husband and wife to be assessed separately and this will be done if requested.

State supplementary benefit

There is now a specified minimum weekly income below which a supplementary benefit can be claimed. The payment is intended to raise the income level, after certain deductions have been made from your actual income to cover basic needs and extra is given to help with rent and rates or, in the case of owner-occupiers, to help with insurance, repairs and similar expenses. If your income falls below the level specified on the form at the back of your pension book then you should send in your claim without delay. This supplement is as much an entitlement as is the basic pension and there is no need to consider it as charity as some mistakenly do. In the nature of things, a means test is a reasonable accompaniment of such aid, since it is intended for those whose real income is below the minimum level that has been set, and which is adjusted from time to time to allow for inflation. For a married couple, their total income is taken into account when assessing the claim.

Those who receive this supplement to their pensions are also entitled to exemption from charges for spectacles, dentures and dental treatment in addition to the exemption from prescription charges which all who are over the statutory retirement ages are entitled to. Local Authorities also operate schemes for rent and rate rebates and provide help over heating costs for persons of limited means. Details of all these helps can be obtained from the local council office or your local Citizens' Advice Bureau. They will also be able to advise you about the special allowances which are now available for the disabled.

Occupational Pension

For many people the pension they receive from

their previous employer will form the major part of their retirement income. Occupational pension schemes vary widely but the actual pension is usually between one half and two-thirds of the salary at retirement. The amount will also vary depending on the years of service and two-thirds is the maximum allowable under government regulations and corresponds to about 40 years of service. The best schemes make some provision for increases to take account of inflation but few are as generous as the index-linked scheme operating for many in the public sector. It is the people on fixed pensions who have been most badly hit by the inflation of recent years.

Most company schemes offer several alternatives to the single straight pension. The most important is that which makes provision for the wife of the pensioner to receive a proportion of the pension for her lifetime if her husband should die first, which, statistically, is the more likely. This usually involves a slight reduction in the pension but, unless some adequate alternative provision has been made, it is a wise and necessary arrangement to adopt.

Some schemes allow for the pension to be taken as one lump sum in lieu and in certain circumstances this may be worth while, but if the pension is inflation-proofed in any way a lump sum is of doubtful value. On the other hand it may be possible to take part as a lump sum with a consequent reduction in the amount of the actual pension. A lump sum might be useful to pay off the whole or part of a mortgage but the various alternatives should be carefully considered well before the actual date of retirement and it is worth getting expert advice so that you may make the best choice depending on your particular circumstances.

For tax purposes your pension will be treated in the same way as your salary has been and the Pension Department will deduct your Income Tax on the Pay-as-you-earn system. So you will only be able to count on the net amount from your occupational pension as expendable income. You will receive your National Retirement Pension without any deduction but the amount will have to be stated on your tax return and will be counted as part of your total income for tax assessment. Whatever we may think about the present levels of taxation, it is comforting to know that thanks to the PAYE system you will not be called upon to pay your tax in one large lump sum

If you are self-employed or are an employer who, under the present regulations, is not permitted to participate in the pension scheme you have set up for your employees, then you will have, or should have, made early provision for your retirement. There are various ways in which this can be done and there are important tax concessions available to help. A Retirement Annuity Policy is an excellent way of making such provision but again it is wise to get expert advice as to what will best be suited to your case.

Investment income

Not everyone is able to put something aside for a rainy day; nor is there quite the same incentive to do so now that better provision is made for retirement by way of pensions and supplementary allowances. Perhaps this is why the policy of so many today is

'Spend as you earn' rather than 'Save as you earn'. Inflation no doubt has something to do with this for we are all very conscious of the way the value of the pound has dropped during the past few years. Despite this, most people would agree that it is wise to have a nest egg which can be drawn upon in an emergency or which will help to augment their income when that takes a cut on retirement.

During the years approaching retirement, income is usually at its peak as the expense of bringing up a family has diminished, and the house mortgage may have been paid off so that then, if not before, is the time to be putting away some savings for the days to come. Maybe an endowment policy has matured or a legacy has come from a deceased relative and the question arises as to how it may best be invested. The days when it would have been put in a box under the bed or hidden in the garden have long since passed! The foolish servant in the parable had to learn that money hidden away and not put to use did nobody any good.

If you are investing before retirement you will probably be interested more in capital appreciation and, after retirement, in income. Much will depend on whether you require to have easy and quick access to your capital or whether you can allow it to be tied up for lengthy periods. Security is usually an important factor and this will rule out the more speculative investments which offer a high reward but carry with them a high risk. Inflation, which seems to have become an almost permanent feature of our economy, is another factor to be kept in mind, so, unless the amount you have to invest is small, it will almost certainly pay you to get expert advice. Your bank manager or accountant may be able to help and there are a number of specialist companies of investment brokers who cater for retired people. Circumstances vary so much that each case needs to be considered on its merits. There are so many ways in which money can be invested that the problem is to choose what is best for you and there may well be several equally good alternatives which different experts will suggest. What I have attempted to do is to outline briefly some of the different ways by which you can put your money to good use and to try to point out their relative advantages and disadvantages. They can be grouped broadly under six main headings.

Government Schemes

National Savings Certificates

There have been a number of different issues of these bearing different rates of interest and the latest (18th) issue offers a simple, safe form of investment for those with small sums to put away occasionally. They can be purchased in £10 units starting with a minimum investment of one and up to a maximum holding of £1,500. They can be cashed at short notice but if this is done within the first four years they yield rather a poor return. So to get the best results they should be kept for a minimum of five years.

There is a special issue of these certificates known as the Index-Linked Retirement Issue available only to men of 65 and over and women of 60 and over. There is a maximum holding of £700 per person. During the first year after purchase repayment will be made only at the purchase price, but thereafter the certificate will be revalued on a monthly basis in accordance with the rise in the Retail Price Index since the purchase date. If the certificate is held for five years its value will be increased by the addition of a bonus at the rate of 4% of the purchase price. At a time of high inflation this is a useful investment for money which is not likely to be required for at least a year. It means that a married couple can invest £1,400 of their savings knowing that it is fully safeguarded against inflation. As the rate of inflation falls so the attractiveness of this as an investment diminishes but it is likely to be some years before other safe investments can compete with it.

Although there is no interest payable on these certificates, the capital appreciation due to their being index linked more than compensates and they are free of tax.

National Savings Bank

This used to be called the Post Office Savings Bank and it has been for years, and continues to be, a simple, safe and convenient method of banking for large numbers of people. The great advantage is that paying in and drawing out can be done through any post office. An ordinary account can be opened with as little as 25p and the top limit is £10,000 per account. Interest accrues at the rate of 4½% (1979) per annum and the first £70 of interest is free of tax.

An investment account is designed for bigger, longer term savings and an account can be opened for as little as £1 with a top limit of £50,000. One month's notice has to be given for withdrawals and the interest accrues at a rate which varies with the Bank Rate. Interest at 12% is subject to tax if your total income is such that you have to pay tax.

Save as you earn (SAYE)

This is a scheme which was introduced to encourage regular savings. Provided they are allowed to accrue for a minimum of five years and preferably seven years, they yield a very attractive tax free return. The scheme is in two parts, one run by the National Savings Bank and the Trustee Savings Banks, and the other by the Building Societies. Up to £20 per month can be contracted with each part so that if husband and wife are both working and can save £80 per month between them this will amount in five years to nearly £5,000, representing a net interest rate of about 8% which is equal to about 12% for those who pay tax at the normal rate. This is quite an attractive investment for those who are preparing for retirement.

British Savings Bonds

These cost £5 each and interest is paid every six months at a rate of 9½% which is liable to income tax. At the end of five years a 4% non-taxable bonus is added as an encouragement to retain them for that period. There is a limit of £10,000 for any one person. They have the advantage that they can be cashed at one month's notice.

Government Stocks

This is a group covering a large number of government issues, mostly Treasury Stocks or Loans with varying rates of interest and repayable at specific dates. They are classed as marketable securities and can be bought and sold like stocks and shares at prices which very according to the state of the money market. Capital gains tax arising from the sale of these stocks is payable only if they are sold within 12 months of their being acquired. Similarly capital losses arising from such sales can only be set against capital gains within the same 12 months period. This is not a field for the small investor except under expert guidance.

Local Authority Bonds

I have included these here under the general group of government schemes as they provide a similar no-risk form of investment with trustee security status. They carry a fixed interest rate and are usually for fixed periods of one or more years. They offer better interest rates than most government stocks but do not have the same capital gains tax exemptions. They are marketable like other securities. Interest is paid every six months and if the term is one year or more the tax is deducted before payment.

Banks

Commercial Banks

As far as most of us are concerned the function of a bank with which we have a current account has more to do with spending than with saving our money. Your current account will not normally earn any interest and may incur bank charges depending on the extent to which you use it and the average amount you keep in it. You can put your money in a deposit account but the interest rate is low comparable with what is obtainable elsewhere; so this is no way to invest your money unless it suits you to use it in the short term to feed your current account.

The banks do provide other services in addition to handling your cheques and a friendly bank manager is useful to turn to for advice on financial problems. If it is an important issue it is always wise, as in medical matters, to get a second opinion if possible from someone else who is knowledgeable in such matters.

Trustee Savings Banks

These were set up initially with the principal emphasis on the savings aspect and, whilst this is still an important part of their business, they have developed more into line with the commercial banks. They operate a cheque account which corresponds with the commercial banks current account. They also have a savings account to encourage regular savings on which there is the same free of tax interest allowance as for the National Savings Bank, and an investment account which yields a higher rate of interest but requires longer notice of withdrawal.

Building societies

These have a good deal to offer especially to those who are in the period leading up to retirement. They offer a number of alternatives from a share account, which carries the minimum interest rate with easy withdrawal facilities to long term shares, two or more years, which carry higher rates of interest. The former account can be opened with as little as £1 and up to £15,000 can be held by one person. It is a convenient way of banking money which you may require at short notice and has the advantage of earning interest all the time. The long-term shares usually have a minimum of £500 with the same maximum as the others.

An important aspect of building society shares is that interest is paid free of tax, unless you pay at the higher tax rates. But anyone on a low income who does not pay tax is at a disadvantage since tax is not reclaimable. This is due to a special arrangement that the societies have with the government over the tax they pay which enables them to pay a higher tax-free interest rate to their members than would otherwise be the case.

Interest rates payable by a building society are liable to vary with changes in the general level of interest rates and are normally about 2½% below the mortgage rates. Money invested in a building society brings in a reasonable return and it is a safe investment, but it does nothing to provide against inflation. Should you want to purchase a house on retirement and need to build up funds in preparation then an account with a building society will give you some priority in the event of your needing to take out a mortgage.

Assurance companies

I am using this term to cover that large group of companies which deal with insurance of both life and property, the term 'assurance' being normally associated with life rather than with property. Car insurance is a legal necessity on which we have no option and most people will accept the need for insurance of their homes and valuables. Not so many see the need for a life assurance policy though it is a wise precaution for anyone to take, especially if there are dependants. None of us can have a guarantee on the length of life we may be able to enjoy and a life policy means that we are sharing the risk with others and providing for those who may be left behind. An excellent way of combining life cover with saving for the future is to take out an endowment policy with a specified maturing date when a capital sum will become due. If a 'with profits' policy is taken out then the capital sum will be increased by the addition of a bonus each year depending on the success of the company's business. Such a policy can be arranged to mature on retirement and this can be one way of investing for retirement as well as gaining life cover.

An important part of assurance companies' business and one which has particular relevance to retirement is that of annuities. For a lump sum payment they will undertake to provide a person with an income for life. This will be greater than would be provided by any other form of investment because the company can afford to use both capital and interest since there is no capital repayment at death. The terms obtainable will vary with the age of the person purchasing the annuity; the older you are the greater it will be since the number of years they are likely to have to pay will be less. Less favourable terms are available for women because their life expectation is rather longer than men.

There are numerous variations on the annuity theme such as a guarantee to pay the income for a minimum number of years which covers the eventuality of death shortly after the start. Provision can also be made for a joint annuity which will continue after one partner has died. Special schemes are also available by which a house owner can capitalize on the value of his property to purchase an annuity with a guarantee that occupancy can continue for life.

As with all other aspects of retirement finance, it pays to get the best advice available and to shop around, for rates vary and some of the companies offer better terms than others. The advantage of an annuity is that it will bring a higher income with less tax deduction since part of it is reckoned as capital repayment and is not taxed. The disadvantage is that the capital is being surrendered for the sake of the income and this may be undesirable if there are dependants.

A retirement annuity policy is an excellent way of providing for a retirement income for those who are self-employed or who are not in any occupational pension scheme. It offers a number of tax advantages and is a good basis for regular saving prior to retirement and for a safe income subsequently. The full amount of the income on this type of policy is subject to tax but, owing to the concessions during the build-up period, there is usually an overall advantage as compared with the lump sum purchase of an annuity. For the self-employed there are also other methods which should be investigated whereby a retirement fund can be built up using the special tax allowances which are granted under present legislation.

Investments made under any of these first four categories may be considered to offer a high degree of security, the only risk being a complete breakdown of the economy which would affect everything else as well. In the next two categories, however, there will be some element of risk which has been demonstrated in recent years when even some large companies of international reputation have failed.

Stocks and shares

The operation of the Stock Exchange is a mystery to the man in the street and the large fluctuations in share prices that occur from time to time seem so remote from ordinary life. Reference is sometimes made to the Stock Exchange as though it was a casino where fortunes were being made and lost in a night! It is true that some fortunes are lost and others made in this way but these are exceptional and it must be recognized that investment in industry, as seen in the issue of stocks and shares, is a vital ingredient in the commercial life of our country. The greater part of the capital invested in industry comes directly or indirectly either from the savings of millions of individuals or from money contributed by them through their employment, e.g. pension fund contributions. In fact by far the larger amount comes from the latter source and reaches the market either by way of purchase of shares or by direct investment by the recipients of these vast sums of money, namely insurance companies and pension funds, and to a lesser extent unit trusts. So, even the man who saves nothing beyond what is paid in towards his occupational pension has a vested interest in the success of the companies whose shares have been bought by his pension fund.

Most stocks and shares are quoted on the stock

market and are available for anyone who has money to invest. A stockbroker will, for a reasonable commission, carry out your instructions to buy and sell. There are some individuals who manage successfully to play the market and make a profit by buying and selling at the appropriate time. There are also some investment clubs where a group of people combine their operations, usually with the help of some experts amongst them, and make a profit (or a loss!) in which they all share. Speculation of this kind has, for some, undesirable undertones of gambling and it is not easy to decide where genuine investment ends and gambling begins. There is no doubt that there is an element of risk in all such operations and it is not a field into which the uninitiated should venture without wise and skilful guidance.

Investment in industry through the purchase of stocks and shares, whilst it carries some risk, does offer some protection against inflation since a company's assets will tend to appreciate in a period of inflation. On the other hand the return on the investment in dividends can vary a great deal depending on the particular market in which it operates. So, to sum it up, direct investment in the stock market is for the few rather than the many.

Unit Trusts

There are now many of these operated by trust companies and the banks. They operate in different fields and each has a wide portfolio of shares in a number of companies. They offer an easy and fairly safe method for the small investor to invest in stocks and shares on a shared basis knowing that the trusts are being managed by experts. Despite this, however, their performance has varied widely and in this field also good advice is essential unless you are an expert yourself.

Property etc

There is a sense in which every house owner is holding an investment in property and there are few better ways of inflation-proofing one's capital. So, to own your own house, even though it involves taking out a mortgage, is seldom other than a very wise move, especially with retirement in view.

Property, as an investment apart from the house you live in, is a different proposition. You pay no income tax on the house you live in, nor are you liable for any capital gains tax if you sell it. But any income from other property is taxable and if you sell it and make a profit then you are likely to have to pay capital gains tax. Property to rent can bring many problems not only over increased costs of maintenance and repairs but over fixed rents and secured tenancies which protect the tenant but often seem to disregard the rights of the landlord. Some folk who have retired to the seaside have put their money into holiday flats or caravans and have found them to be a profitable investment. They may be suitable for some people but, as with any other investment, do get good advice before rushing into it.

I know some people who have put their spare money, not into bricks and mortar but into valuables such as antiques, works of art, coins, jewellery, stamps and other collectors' items. Over the past ten years there has been a phenomenal increase in the value of such things and those who possess them and have held them for some time could now sell them at greatly enhanced prices. As a field of profitable investment, however, this is likely to be limited to those who have the specialized knowledge and skill necessary to tell the genuine from the fake. I would not want to discourage the keen collector whether it be of cigarette cards or chimney pots! Collecting can be a source of much enjoyment and interest, but only exceptionally is it a hobby that will add much to the income. The possession of a valuable antique can bring much pleasure and satisfaction as its value appreciates but its monetary value appears only when you sell it, and it is vulnerable to theft and damage in a way that money invested in other ways is not.

Your expenditure

Having established at least your basic retirement income, which will consist of your National Retirement and your occupational pensions, you will then be faced with the problem of balancing your budget. Income is not too difficult to assess but to estimate your expenditure is not so easy. Some of your expenses will be reduced, some are likely to increase and others will remain much the same as before. Let us consider them in these three categories.

Reduced Costs

Income Tax

This is now a major item in most budgets and it is the reduction in tax which is most helpful in retirement. First of all you can reckon on an immediate tax reduction of the order of one third of the drop in your income since the whole of this will probably come off your taxable income. Then if you are over 65, there will be a further reduction due to the increased age allowance, a figure which is adjusted upwards each time the retirement pension is increased. For a married couple the age exemption is allowed if either spouse is over 65 but there is an upper limit of income above which the extra age allowance is gradually reduced to the standard figure. Also for those over 65 there is a higher level of investment income permitted before the surcharge is applied. These three reductions go a considerable way towards minimising the effect of your drop in income when you retire.

Other reductions

Immediately you start to receive your National Retirement Pension you no longer have to pay any National Insurance contributions so this represents a further useful saving.

For many people travelling to work, especially if you are a commuter living some distance away from your job, travelling costs can be substantial, so this will be another valuable reduction in your expenses. As a pensioner you will be eligible for various travel concessions both in rail and coach travel; British

Rail sell a special pass for pensioners which enables you to get cheap travel all over the system. If you have to do much train travelling this will save you a great deal. You may be in an area where cheap bus passes or even free tickets are available.

Another area of saving is in house repairs and decorating. In my own case, being a DIY enthusiast, I have always done a great deal of such work myself so there has not been much saving as far as I am concerned. But others who may not have had time to do this work in the past will find that retirement gives both the time and the incentive to tackle these jobs with substantial savings in cost.

There is every encouragement these days to 'do-it-yourself' with materials and tools specially designed for the amateur so that there can be few men and women not able to take on at least the simpler jobs inside the house. It is at the same time a satisfying and profitable occupation and the saving is substantial when you consider that only about one-fifth of the total cost is for materials and the rest is labour and overhead expenses.

You will probably hope to continue having the same sort of holidays as before and you will find that there are many offers at reduced prices if you will take your holiday in the spring or the autumn, keeping clear of the busy summer months and the crowds. My wife and I have enjoyed some happy spring holidays with SAGA, a travel company which organizes holidays at home and abroad for the over-60s. Other holiday companies have special offers for pensioners so you should be able to enjoy your holidays still at reasonable cost.

Medical prescriptions are free for pensioners and, whilst we all hope to avoid having to take medicines of any kind, there are times when it is necessary and, for those who are under continuous medication, cutting out the prescription charge is a real saving.

There are many minor ways in which further savings will be effected. Traders often offer concessions to pensioners as for example in hairdressing and dry-cleaning. Entrance fees to cinemas, museums and similar places are often reduced and subscriptions to clubs and organizations are usually less for senior citizens. In our town the council even provide free tickets to enable us to use the deck chairs along the promenade.

Increased costs

I have not mentioned food costs so far and for some there may be an increase here when there have been luncheon vouchers or subsidized canteen meals. On the other hand those who have to pay the full price for restaurant meals may well find that lunch for two at home costs less than before and they may save on this item.

Heating and lighting costs may perhaps increase as the house will be more occupied than before and extra electric power, or gas, will be required for the mid-day meal for two instead of one.

From personal experience I would say that there are very few increased costs consequent on retirement and we have found no difficulty in adjusting our expenditure to fit our retirement income without in any way feeling that we were any worse off on account of it.

Up or down or much the same

Other major expenses, not so far mentioned, will depend very much on individual circumstances. The principal items are:

The house

If you are staying put then there will be little change as rent, rates, mortgage and insurance will, apart from inflation which affects everything alike, remain much the same. As already pointed out, it should be possible to reduce the maintenance costs by carrying out some of the repairs and redecorating yourself.

If you are moving to another house, it will probably be smaller and less expensive unless you go to a popular seaside town and live in a bungalow, when you may find that it costs you more. This is more likely to happen if you move from North to South. When we retired from Manchester and came to a South Coast town we exchanged our four bedroomed family house for a two bedroomed bungalow for about the same price and found that the rates and expenses were about the same as for the larger house.

The car

If you have not had a car then this will be no problem and it is unlikely that you will want to start to drive after retirement. If you have been using your car for business or for getting to your job then you will benefit from the lower mileage and maintenance costs especially if you are able to tackle the simple maintenance jobs yourself. The basic costs of licensing and insurance will not change and if you stop to calculate the cost per mile of your pleasure motoring you may be horrified! It is a luxury indeed, but one that many would be loth to give up as they use their cars for family visits and for ferrying other people about to church or elsewhere. In fact the car might be counted one of the necessary luxuries of life.

Clothes

As in the case of food, basic costs are not likely to change much, but if you have been in a job where you had to be smartly dressed or conversely where your clothes wore out quickly, then you may find that this is another item where you can save money.

Your giving

This is a subject that I have not yet seen mentioned in any book that I have read on the topic of retirement finance and yet giving is an integral part of Christian faith and practice as it is, indeed, of other faiths. The setting aside of one tenth of their money, or tithing as it is termed, was a solemn obligation to the Jews and so scrupulous were some that they applied tithing even to the herbs grown in their gardens. Similarly for many Christians the practice of setting aside one tenth at least of their take home pay to give away and not to spend on themselves is a lifelong principle. I have yet to meet anyone who does this who has not experienced the truth of the wise word in Ecclesiastes 11:1: 'Cast your bread upon the waters, for you will find it after many days.' Or as a friend of mine quaintly used to put it, '... and it will come back to you as ham sandwiches!' Not that our motive should be that of profiting materially from it but rather the New Testament principle that 'it is more blessed to give than to receive' and the exhortation, 'Freely you have received, freely give.'

I have heard it said that because of their drop in income, retired people cannot be expected to give as generously as they used to do. But experience shows that those who give generously continue to do so whatever their income, and many manage to maintain the same level of giving as before. The story of the widow's mite in Mark 12 illustrates this point.

So much for the principle of giving: what about the practice? The allocation of our gifts is entirely a personal matter. We all have our favourite charities and there is no lack of them, nor of the need for them despite the vast increase in the services provided by the welfare state. Even if there is now less need for charity in our own country, the needs of the Third World call for our practical help all the time. The support of the church will be a primary responsibility of its members and this has long been recognized by non-conformists. The Church of England has for too long relied on past benefactors and only now, due to the pressure of inflation, are its members beginning to give the necessary support to maintain its work and ministry.

With rather more time available after retirement it is a good thing to organize your giving with the same care as you give to the rest of your expenditure. Some give casually or on impulse whereas all giving should be with due deliberation and thought so that what you give is put to the best possible use.

For many years I used to support a particular charitable fund which had been set up to help people in need who belonged to my profession. I used to receive the annual report and accounts but never bothered to study them in detail. After I retired I took a close look at the next report and discovered that administration costs had risen so high that one third of what was being given was being used to distribute the remainder. This compared very badly with some similar charities that I knew so I protested about it to the Board of Management. I was a lone individual and my protest got me nowhere; so all I could do was to withdraw my support. I suggest that you take an interest in those charities which you support and study their reports and accounts, taking special note of their administrative costs and reserve funds. After all, the subscriber pays the piper and he ought to be able to call the tune! We have a responsibility to give and also a responsibility to ensure that our gifts are used to the best advantage in the cause which we support. If we view seriously our stewardship of money, then we shall use it responsibly both in what we are spending on ourselves and what we give to others.

There are certain matters connected with giving that call for special comment.

Covenants

Although some have questioned the ethics of this system whereby some of our income tax can be reclaimed for charitable use, it is generally accepted that this is a provision under the income tax law which rightly can and should be used to the full. The amount involved in relation to total taxation is small but it is an important ingredient in the finances of most charities, including churches, missionary societies, and such like.

When he enters into a covenant, the donor undertakes to pay, usually for a seven-year period (normally, but not necessarily ceasing on his death) an annual sum which is usually a fixed amount. It can, however, be fixed in relation to a number of factors: e.g. it could be increased annually by the increase in the official cost of living index. The effect of such a convenant is that the net amount given each year is grossed up at the standard rate of income tax and the charity is able to recover the income tax in question as it would on a dividend from one of its investments. The amount of the gift is thereby increased by some 50% without any extra cost to the donor. The income of the covenantor must be such that, after deducting all his allowances, he is paying at the standard rate on an amount which is not less than the grossed total of any covenants (or other annual charges) that he may have on his income.

There are several variations to the covenant scheme which are worth mentioning. There is what is known as a 'funded' covenant in which a lump sum is paid to a charity on the understanding that it is an interest free loan of which one seventh is taken each year as a covenanted gift on which income tax can be reclaimed. If death occurs before the covenant runs out, it will lapse so it is wise to make provision beforehand for the remainder to be dealt with either as a legacy to the charity or to be repaid to the estate.

Another method is to set up your own trust to which you covenant to pay a regular amount and from which you can allocate the money, which will include the income tax recovered, to charity as you wish. It involves a simple trust deed for which you need to get some professional help, and a separate bank account which will deal with the incoming and outgoing payments. You need to keep a careful account of the trust funds, which is not at all difficult, and a return has to be made annually claiming the appropriate refund. My wife and I did this some years ago and we seek to channel a considerable part of our giving in this way. We are ourselves the trustees and decide how the funds are to be disbursed. The advantage of this scheme is that it avoids having a number of different covenants on each of which the charity concerned has to make a claim and it gives us complete control of the giving which, of course, must be done within the terms of the trust. It would not, for example, be possible to set up a trust out of which you paid for your own holidays!

A rather similar scheme which involves a minimum of trouble on your part is to make a covenant with one of the specialist charitable trusts and they will administer your gift for a small commission. You will be able to specify how your money is to be distributed, including the tax reclaimed. If you want to donate a lump sum, then that can be handled similarly to the funded covenant previously mentioned.

So far I have only considered covenants in the context of gifts to church or charitable funds. They are not limited to these but can be used in other ways. For example, grandparents can covenant a gift to help towards the cost of education of their grandchildren and tax can be recovered on the gift. Professional advice should be sought as to the extent to which you can amplify your giving by using covenants in other ways.

Capital transfer tax

This tax is charged on the decrease in value of any of your net assets which you suffer as a result of any transfer of these other than for full value and whether or not this happens during your lifetime or at your death.

The total of any transfers during lifetime are, however, cumulative and the amount payable on the balance of your assets at death calculated accordingly. However, lower rates apply to lifetime gifts than those passing on death but any gifts within the last three years of your life are treated as if they had been made on death. So don't leave it too late! There are, however, certain exceptions which are as follows:

• Transfers between your wife and yourself both during your lives and on death are exempt from the tax and this gives appreciable scope for re-arrangement of your affairs with a view to minimising the liability. In particular no capital transfer tax is payable on the death of a spouse who dies first insofar as he or she has left any property to the surviving spouse either absolutely or for a life interest.

• Outright gifts to any one person not exceeding £100 for any fiscal year (ending 5th April) are exempt.

• Any person (including husband and wife) can transfer assets of a value not exceeding £2,000 in every fiscal year. This means that a married couple can give up to £4,000 per year to their children if this is possible and desirable.

- There is also exemption for what is called normal expenditure out of income. For purposes of tax, these words are interpreted as to mean a regular gift out of your income (after tax) such that it does not in any way affect your normal standard of living. Life insurance premiums are particularly suited to come under this exemption.
- Gifts in consideration of marriage are also exempt up to a maximum of £5,000 if the donor is a parent of one of the marriage partners; £2,500 if a grandparent or great grandparent or one of the parties themselves. Otherwise such a gift is limited to £1,000.
- As regards charities the present law allows any gifts made to them during lifetime to be free of Capital Transfer Tax except for those made within one year of death or given under a will where the limit is £100,000.

As regards the payment of tax, the first £25,000 for any one person is free of tax and the tax is then levied on a scale starting at a comparatively low rate and finishing at 75% on very large estates.

In view of the lower rates for lifetime transfers it is very important that these exemptions should be used to the greatest advantage i.e. normally during life, but the whole matter is so complicated that if there is any possibility of liability, professional advice should be taken, as this can result in very considerable savings of this particular duty. The figures given above show the position obtaining in 1978 and may be changed in later years.

10
WILLS AND BEREAVEMENT

He will wipe away all tears from their eyes: there shall be an end to death, and to mourning and crying and pain. (Revelation 21:4)

At first sight these two topics may seem to be strange bedfellows but both are closely related to the universal fact of death. A will is a practical business provision which comes into operation at death; bereavement is an emotional and psychological result of a death. In our modern world, which boasts of its freedom to discuss anything without restraint or censorship, death is usually, as a recent book title suggests, 'The last thing we talk about'. There almost seems to be a conspiracy of silence on the whole subject even though we accept that it is a fact of life. So let us look at these two diverse but related subjects.

Wills

Just as many are reluctant to talk about death, so much the same attitude is taken over the making of a will which is put off and put off until it is too late. Somehow there is a feeling that to think about your will is to show a morbid attitude to life and almost to invite an early demise! This can only be described as superstitious nonsense!

It is a wise and necessary thing to do in any case, but especially if you have any dependants for whom provision has to be made in the event of your death. Under English law anyone from the age of 18 can make a will regardless of the amount of the estate, which is the legal term used to cover any money, property or personal possessions. The essential elements of a will are very simple. It comprises a document as follows: 1. You state your wishes as to how your estate should be distributed after your death. 2. You appoint one or more executors to administer it. 3. You sign it in the presence of two witnesses who must also sign it in your presence and in the presence of each other.

There are certain simple provisions such as requiring that the two witnesses and their spouses must be other than those to whom you may be leaving anything in the will. Adequate provision for dependants should be made otherwise it is possible for them to contest the will afterwards and have it altered. The intention of the legislation which allows this is to safeguard the position of, for example, a wife, so that she cannot be 'cut off with a shilling' as has been known to happen in the past.

The wording of a will must be clear and unequivocal so that there can be no misunderstanding as to what was intended. All too often ambiguous wording in a will has led to family upsets and conflicts and to expensive litigation.

You may well ask why, if the making of a will is so simple, it is ever necessary to employ a solicitor to do the job for you and to word it in legal jargon which the layman finds so difficult to follow. Where the estate is large and in any way complicated, or where family trusts are involved, it is advisable to get expert help over the wording. This will minimise the danger of misunderstanding arising in winding up the estate. A do-it-yourself will is perfectly possible for the person with modest means and an uncomplicated estate but even so it is wise to get some advice from a knowledgeable friend or from one of the various books that are now available. One of the best I know is entitled *Wills and Probate* and is published by the Consumers Association. This gives valuable information on all the aspects of drawing up a will and also explains how the executor has to do his job. It also explains certain important differences between English and Scottish law as regards wills.

Here again there is no reason why your executor, provided he has some business experience, cannot, without calling in other help, administer the will and obtain probate, which is the legal term for the official permission to proceed to carry out the requirements of the will. However, if there are any complications, then it may be advisable for him to enlist the aid of a solicitor who is experienced in this work. Alternatively, the job of executor can be carried out by a bank or the Public Trustee who can then be named in the will. They will, of course, charge for their services and this will be a prior charge on the estate. If the executor is a friend or relative, then it is permissible to make a bequest to him in the will.

From time to time you should review your will to take account of changes in your circumstances and for minor changes a simple codicil is adequate. This is a further document which refers to the original will and states that it is the first or subsequent alteration to it. It must be signed and witnessed in exactly the same way as the will itself. Should major changes be required, then it is best to make out a new will. When anyone marries, a will made before the marriage is automatically revoked and a new will is necessary, except when it is specifically stated that it is 'in consideration of marriage'.

There is no legal obligation to make a will and there are many who, for one reason or another, fail to do so and in the legal term 'die intestate'. In such a case, the next of kin usually has to apply for Letters of Administration which is the equivalent of Probate for a will. This enables the estate to be wound up but it has to be done quite arbitrarily, and there is often much trouble, expense and delay over it, and the services of a solicitor may be necessary. By making a will in good time, you can avoid all this and ensure that your wishes are carried out and your dependents properly provided for.

The need to make adequate provision for dependants such as a wife, an unmarried daughter or young or handicapped children is obvious and these should always be given priority in a will. But quite often when the family has grown up and the children have become independent financially, and possibly even better off than their parents, there may no longer be the same need for them to expect all their parents' money to be left to them. The time of need is usually greatest in the early days of bringing up a family and gifts from parents can then be much more useful than legacies after death. Nor should it be taken for granted that, regardless of circumstances, all the parents' estate should be left to their family. There is so much need in the world and so many worthy causes need support that a sharing out, where possible before rather than after death, and according to need is worthy of careful consideration. Of course everything depends on relative circumstances which will vary in every case so that there can be no general rule to apply. The current legislation under the Capital Transfer Act, which was dealt with in Chapter 9, is an added incentive to take what surely is a wise course of action.

Other matters

There are certain practical matters, apart from the will, in which it is usual for the next of kin or an executor to be involved immediately following a death. The first step is to obtain from the deceased's doctor a certificate stating the cause of death. When issuing this, the doctor will also provide a formal notice stating that he has signed this certificate. If the death has been sudden or unexpected, or has been due to some unnatural cause such as an accident, then the circumstances have to be reported to the coroner who will then decide whether a post mortem is needed to establish the cause of death, and whether an inquest will have be held. Once the coroner has been involved, it is necessary to obtain his permission before the funeral can take place.

Then, within five days of the death, the local registrar of births and deaths must be notified of the death. He will need the doctor's certificate referred to above, and, if possible, also the deceased's National Health Service medical card. Provided the coroner is not involved, the registrar will issue a certificate of disposal which enables the funeral to take place. He will also provide a special death certificate for Health Insurance purposes. Other certificates can also be obtained from him for claims upon life insurance and similar policies.

The cost of the funeral constitutes a first charge on the estate as do also any legal charges concerned with the administration of the will. So it is wise to obtain an estimate for the funeral and to make sure that the cost is such as the deceased would have approved and can be met either by the estate or with help from family or friends. Funerals can be expensive and the death grant (currently £30) paid by the Department of Health and Social Security does not go very far towards it.

Death duties have been replaced by the capital transfer tax which is a very complicated system of taxation already referred to in Chapter 9. It depends not merely on the value of the estate but takes into account also certain gifts made during one's lifetime. If the estate is such that it is likely to be subject to C.T. Tax, then it is advisable to obtain advice from a bank manager, accountant or solicitor.

A useful leaflet entitled *Practical Problems Following a Death,* which deals in more detail with these and other associated matters is obtainable from your local Citizens' Advice Bureau, or directly from the National Council of Social Service.

Try to leave your affairs in good order so that your executor can readily find out all the necessary details without having to search through a mass of files and papers. It is a good plan at intervals to make out a list giving all the important references such as your Bank Account number and any other accounts, your assets such as share certificates, and details of any valuables you may possess. Your house deeds and other important documents, including your will, can be stored with your bank for safety. These may seem to be elementary precautions but put yourself in the shoes of someone who will one day have the task of administering your estate, whether it be small or large, and do your best to make it as simple as possible for him.

Whilst on this subject, it is wise to leave instructions, which preferably should be apart from your will in a separate document, regarding your funeral. You may wish to be buried and not cremated, and then this should be stated in writing so that all concerned may be aware of it. There is also the question of flowers at the funeral. It is much more satisfactory if your friends are told beforehand whether or not flowers are to be sent. Often these days flowers are limited to the immediate family and the name of a charity is given so that friends may make a gift to that as a more lasting tribute to your memory, and that is an excellent plan. You can also give any other instructions regarding favourite hymns or readings for your funeral service.

Some people may wish their eyes to be donated for corneal grafting (and these can be used regardless of age) or their bodies given for medical research. Any such wishes should be clearly stated in their instructions.

It greatly helps if your doctor is aware of your wishes in this connection so that a note can be made on your medical record file. He will then, without delay, be able to seek for formal approval from your next of kin before taking action.

Bereavement

Death

There must be few of us who do not, during the course of our lives, encounter bereavement when death comes to take away someone near and dear to us. It may be a loved parent or a close friend; but no loss can be greater than that of a marriage partner with whom one has shared the greater part of a lifetime. In retirement, those of us who are married must face the fact that almost certainly one partner will die before the other. Due to the greater expectation of life of women, and also because wives are usually younger than their husbands, it is likely that it will be the wife who will suffer this bereavement.

The ideal marriage is one in which the husband and wife grow closer together as they grow older and as, with the increasing weakness of old age, they become more and more dependent on each other. So, when one partner dies, the bereavement can be all the more distressing when death disrupts the whole pattern of life that they have built up over the years. This becomes an even more traumatic experience if the likelihood of this happening has not been faced up to frankly beforehand.

This failure to face the fact of death is understandable in the case of those who think of it as a leap in the dark, and who look upon it as the snuffing out of a candle, the end of life and hope. The philosophy of many is quite simple, 'Let us eat, drink and be merry, for tomorrow we die'. But, for the Christian, there is an entirely different outlook, and the well-known words which form part of the funeral service express this very clearly. Jesus said 'I am the Resurrection and the Life; he that believeth in Me, though he were dead, yet shall he live' (John 11:25). It was because of this certain hope that Paul was able to write to the Corinthians: 'O death, where is thy sting? O grave, where is thy victory?' However, despite this fundamental difference in the contemplation of death, bereavement brings grief, sorrow and loss to all concerned regardless of whether they have a Christian faith or not. So let us consider the three stages, before, during and after a bereavement.

Before it happens

Just as it is necessary to prepare for life and for retirement, so there is every reason why we should all be prepared for death. There are the practical matters which have been dealt with in the preceding section, such as the making of a will. It is unkind to those who are left behind if we have not done everything possible to make the task of clearing up our affairs as easy for them as is possible. It may be more difficult for someone in the prime of life to take such steps when many years of life seem to stretch ahead but in our later years when we know that life is reaching its natural term, to get ready for it should be seen as a perfectly normal act.

It should be a subject that husband and wife, or two friends who live together, can discuss quite openly so that, which ever one may die first, the other will be fully prepared for all that has to be done when it happens. To face the fact of bereavement beforehand will not eliminate the shock and the grief which comes as the immediate and natural reaction to it; but you will be braced for it and be better able to endure it.

When it comes to you

We are constantly being reminded of death as we hear and read of others who have passed on, and as, from time to time, we attend the funeral of a friend. We share in their grief and write letters of condolence to those who survive them; but the reality of bereavement only really dawns on us when it comes to us personally. When a child or a parent, or the partner of our marriage is taken from us then, what we have observed with a slight air of detachment suddenly strikes home to us.

The first effect is usually one of *shock*. Even though there has been a long illness, the person has been alive and with us, maybe with some prospect of getting better. Then, suddenly, the end has come; there is no longer the presence of our loved one; there is only the dead body; and the finality of it comes as a terrible blow. At first we may not even be prepared to accept it and we may find ourselves in a severe state of distress as the truth of it slowly dawns on us. We see an example of this in the case of David when he received news of his son Absalom's death. We read that he was overcome with grief and wept and cried 'O Absalom my son! My son Absalom! Absalom my son! If only I had died in your place, my son! Absalom my son!

Following the shock, there can be a period of *numbness*, when life without the loved one seems hardly worth living, and the mind cannot grapple with all the problems that immediately emerge. This is the time when help is most needed and the presence of family or friends who are able to take over in planning the funeral and other necessary arrangements is invaluable.

During this first stage of shock and numbness, the person who has been bereaved should not be expected to make any important decisions, but should be allowed to live a day at a time until the funeral is over. If there is someone on the spot to take over the running of the house, the preparation of the meals and caring for any visitors, then so much the better.

Bereavement is usually, but not always, the occasion for *distress and grief.* When death comes after a painful illness, and has long been expected, then the reaction may well be one of relief and death can be looked upon as a happy release. But even in such circumstances there can be problems of readjustment to the new situation especially if the loss is that of a spouse or a close friend.

At one time it was usual to rely heavily for comfort at the time of a bereavement on one's minister, who was expected to be experienced in helping those who were passing through times of trouble or loss. Today, when so many have no close church connections, it is often the doctor who has to try to help those who have been bereaved, as he is the person on the spot at the time. But normally he is too busy to be able to give the time which a minister might be expected to devote to talking and praying with the survivor. So it is here that close friends can help to give the understanding support that is needed immediately after a death has occurred. Those who have themselves experienced bereavement are best fitted to fill this role and it is at such a time that real friendship, often too deep for words, is most appreciated.

Afterwards

The initial shock and the numbness passes when the funeral is over, when the relatives and friends have left, and the reality of the loss has been brought home to the one who remains. In some parts of the world the funeral is an occasion for much demonstration of mourning and grief in which others besides those immediately involved also take part. This display of feelings can have a beneficial effect on the mourners which is denied them in the more restrained atmosphere of an English funeral. No longer do we see women in widow's weeds which they wore for months afterwards, or men with black armbands showing that they had lost a loved one. The result of this lack of any outward display of mourning tends to be a bottling up of the grief until after the funeral. Then in the quietness and loneliness of the home the full extent of the loss becomes apparent. This is often the most difficult time of all, and it is at this stage that the maximum of help and support is needed; and probably for quite a long time afterwards. There may be a period of apathy or despair, when life seems too difficult to cope with alone. For some there may be a period of depression brought on by the loneliness compounding the grief. There may be feelings of blame or regret in which, quite irrationally, there are thoughts of what might have been done, by oneself or by others, that might have prevented the death.

Grief, working itself out in these and other ways, may last for some months or even years before the readjustment is complete. Much depends on the mentality of the person concerned, and this is where those who have faced the possibility beforehand are so much better able to cope with it when the time comes. And this is where a real Christian faith can draw upon a strength that comes from God, a power beyond ourselves that makes life again worth living and gives meaning even to sorrow and loss; when the promise to the disciples comes to us anew, 'Lo, I am with you always.'

During these difficult days of adjustment, much also depends on the support of family and friends. The older we get the harder it is to adapt to a new way of life and bereavement usually means that we have to do just that when we begin to live alone for the first time, or have to move into an old people's home. It will be true to say that life will never be the same again; but the life we are given is for living today, not yesterday. At the funeral it was natural that there should be grief and tears. Jesus wept at the grave of Lazarus, so tears at the death of a loved one should never be repressed. But the Psalmist reminds us that 'Weeping may endure for a night but joy cometh in the morning'. Psalm 30:5. If we believe that those who die are at rest, that they are freed from pain and suffering, and they share with us the glorious hope of the resurrection of the dead to eternal life, then there should be a finite end to grieving.

Dr F W Boreham, in one of his delightful essays entitled 'Getting over things', puts it like this: 'Time is a great healer. His touch is so gentle that the poor patient is not conscious of its pressure. The days pass, and the weeks, and the months, and the years. Like the trees that start from the rocky faces, and the ferns that creep out of every cranny in the ruined horizon, new interests steal imperceptibly into life. There come new faces, new loves, new thoughts, and new sympathies. The heart responds to fresh influences and bravely declines to die. And whilst the days that are dead are embalmed in costliest spices and lie in the most holy place of the temple of memory, the soul discovers with surprise that it has surmounted the cruel shock of earlier shipwreck and can once more greet the sea.'

A charming poem by L C Jack has been a great help to many who have come to the final stage of bereavement that we have been considering.

When day is done and in the golden west
  My soul from yours sinks slowly out of sight,
  And you alone enjoy the warmth and light
That once had seemed of all God's gifts the best;
When roses bloom and I not there to name,
  When thrushes sing and I not there to hear,
  When rippling laughter breaks upon your ear
And friends come flocking as of old they came –
I pray, dear heart, for sweet remembrance sake
You pluck the rose and hear the songful thrush,
With laughter meet once more the merry jest
And greet familiar faces still awake;
For I, asleep in the eternal hush,
Would have you ever at your golden best.

11
AND WHAT THEN?

So teach us to number our days that we may apply our hearts unto wisdom. (Psalm 90:12)

The title of this chapter was inspired by a story that I have heard more than once and which you may have heard too; but it makes its point so effectively that it will bear repeating. A young man went up to college and was having his first interview with his tutor. 'Well,' said the tutor, 'What are your plans?' 'I intend to work hard and get a good degree,' came the prompt reply. 'And what then?' the tutor asked. 'With a good degree, I should be able to get a job with excellent prospects and when I've saved enough money I expect to settle down and get married.' 'Good,' said the tutor, 'And what then?' By this time the young man was beginning to wonder where the conversation was leading but it was his first interview with his tutor so he felt he must go along with him. 'I hope I shall make a success of my career and have a happy family life,' he replied. 'Excellent,' said the tutor, 'and what then?' The student now began to be really anxious about the continued questioning so he tried to finish it off by saying, 'I suppose, in time, I shall retire and I shall hope to have enough money to live on comfortably until I die.' But the tutor had not finished and again came the question, 'And what then?' But the young man had no reply this time. Death was for him, as it is for so many, a subject that he would rather not think about.

I have taken pains to read as many books as I have been able to lay my hands on which deal with retirement and old age. There has been an interesting variation in their approach to the subject and I have enjoyed some more than others. A good deal of useful and interesting information was to be found in all of them though I have not always agreed with the views expressed. What has struck me very forcibly is that many of them have viewed death, if they have mentioned it at all, as the end of everything and the grave as the final 'full stop'. Some do mention religion as something in which old people may find some comfort, rather viewing it as an optional extra for the elderly which can do them no harm and may possibly do some good.

I have endeavoured throughout this book to stress the value of a positive Christian faith in considering retirement and this applies equally in considering death. For the Christian, death is not the end of life but the beginning of a new and fuller life; not the drawing of the final curtain on the stage of life but the opening of a door to the life beyond. It is not a vague and shadowy prospect of a life of some sort beyond the grave but the sure and certain hope of a resurrection to eternal life. The earthly body dies but the soul, the real person that lived in the body, lives on. This is the Christian hope, the Christian faith. As Paul puts it so clearly in 1 Corinthians 15:19, 20 (Living Bible): 'If being a Christian is only of value to us now in this life, we are the most miserable of creatures. But the fact is that Christ did actually rise from the dead, and he became the first of millions now dead who will come back to life again some day.'

In writing this book I have tried very hard to avoid preaching a sermon so I hope, if you have borne with me thus far, that you will go on to the end. No one would question the need to prepare for life when we are young. The child at school, the student at college, the apprentice at work – it is taken for granted that their preparation is a necessary part of life. I myself have been trying to stress the need to prepare also for that final stage of earthly life that is to be spent in retirement. That too has a finite limit and must some day come to an end. When I get the monthly journal of a technical institution to which I belong, I usually glance through the obituary notices to see if I recognize any of the names there and from time to time I note the passing of some contemporary of mine. Every such name is a timely reminder to me that one day my name is likely to appear there too. But it will be for me not just an end but a new beginning. Can you look forward in that way?

This book was conceived as a sharing of my experience with others who have retired or are coming up to retirement. My hope is that I have been able to pass on something of value to others that will help them to enjoy their retirement as much as I am enjoying mine. It has been something of a personal testimony and, as I said at the beginning, it inevitably reflects my faith as a committed Christian. When I was quite a young man, a business friend of mine, who was an agnostic and with whom I had been discussing my faith, remarked to me, 'I envy you your peace of mind.' He had come to know me quite well and he recognized that I had an inner peace to which he was a stranger. There is a serenity that comes from a personal faith in Jesus Christ and I would be more than happy if I felt that some who read this book and lack that serenity might come to know the peace and joy which I have known, since, as a boy, I committed myself to Jesus Christ as Lord of my life. Perhaps some who have patiently read through to this point may wish that they too could have the simple faith which has been so much a part of my life. They may feel, however, that it has been easy for me after my childhood in a Christian home and an early experience of conversion to live the life of a Christian and to have so confident hope of the life to come. But is it not too late for those who have reached their closing years without any such experience ever to find that same peace and hope? Most certainly not! The love of God, demonstrated to the world by our Lord Jesus Christ, both in his life of service and in his atoning death on the cross for us, is for all, regardless of age, who are willing to accept it. It is not something that we inherit or achieve by our own efforts but, as Paul expressed it in his letter to the Romans (6:23): 'The gift of God is eternal life through Jesus Christ our Lord.' It calls for a personal commitment, an acknowledgement of our sinfulness and our need of forgiveness and a turning to God in simple faith. There are numerous books explaining more fully the way of faith and I commend one that has been a help to many entitled *Peace with God* by Billy Graham.

This chapter, and with it this book, must draw to a close. It will have fulfilled its purpose if, in some small way, it has helped those who read it to find, as I have done, that the years of retirement are indeed bonus years, which are given us to use and to enjoy to the full. I would like to end with the well-known words of Tennyson's poem:

Sunset and evening star,
  And one clear call for me!
And may there be no moaning at the bar,
  When I put out to sea,

But such a tide as moving seems asleep,
  Too full for sound and foam,
When that which drew from out the boundless deep
  Turns again home.

Twilight and evening bell,
  And after that the dark!
And may there be no sadness of farewell
  When I embark;

For, though from out our bourne of time and place
  The flood may bear me far,
I hope to see my Pilot face to face
  When I have crost the bar.

APPENDIX OF USEFUL REFERENCES

APPENDIX OF USEFUL REFERENCES

The addresses of some organizations which are chiefly concerned with retirement and old age together with some others mentioned in this book are given here for easy reference. The list makes no attempt to cover all the organizations concerned since the number is very large; a full list will be found in the copy of *Charities Digest* which will probably be available in your local library.

Many organizations publish helpful literature and reference is given to some of the typical publications; for full details of all their current booklets application should be made to the address given, preferably enclosing a stamped addressed envelope.

Literature relating to retirement is now quite extensive and your local library will probably have a good selection; any special books can usually be obtained for you from one of the central libraries. For official leaflets on matters such as pensions, taxation, allowances and such like, you should apply to the appropriate local or government offices or the Citizens Advice Bureau.

Name & Address	*Concerned with*	*Some Publications*
The Abbeyfield Society, 35a High St., Potters Bar, Herts	Sheltered Housing	—
Age Concern, 60 Pitcairn Rd., Mitcham, Surrey	Welfare	'The Care of Old People.' 'Old People's Welfare Committees.' etc.

British Association of Retired Persons, 14 Frederick St., Edinburgh EH2 2HB	Welfare	—
British Red Cross Society, 9 Grosvenor Crescent, London SW1	Welfare and relief	—
British Voluntary Services Overseas, 10 Belgrave Sq., London SW1	Work abroad	—
Central Council for the Disabled, 34 Eccleston Sq., London SW1V 1PF	Welfare	Various publications for the disabled.
Christians Abroad, 38 King St., London WC2E 8JT	Work abroad	—
Christian Aid, P.O. Box 1, London SW1W 9BW	Overseas relief	—
Consumers' Association 14 Buckingham St., London WC2N 6DS	Publications	'Health for Old Age' 'Which? Way to Slim' 'Where to Live after Retirement' 'Wills and Probate' 'What to do when someone Dies' etc.
Daily Telegraph Information Service, 135 Fleet St., London EC4P 4BL	Publications	'Guide to Retirement'* 'Working for Yourself' etc. (* Contains

		comprehensive reference section)
Disabled Living Foundation, 346 Kensington High St., London W14 8NS	Welfare	Numerous publications for the disabled.
The Employment Fellowship, Drayton House, Gordon St., London WC1H 0BE	Jobs	—
Help the Aged, 8–10 Denman St., London W1A 2AP	Welfare	'Cry and you Cry Alone' 'The Case for Day Centres' etc.
The Housing Corporation, 149 Tottenham Court Rd., London W1P 0BN	Housing	—
Interservice, 19 Draycott Place, London SW3 2SJ	Work Overseas	—
National Council of Social Service, 26 Bedford Sq., London WC1 (includes National Citizens' Advice Bureau Council)	Welfare	'Someone like you can Help'. 'Voluntary Social Service' etc.
National Institute for Adult Education, 35 Queen Anne St., London W1N 8BY	Education	'Year book of Adult Education' 'Calendar of Residential Short Courses'. etc.
The Pre-Retirement Association, 19 Undine St., London SW17 8PP	Retirement preparation and publications	'*Choice*' (monthly magazine). Various kits

		of literature for retirement, etc.
SAGA Senior Citizens' Holidays, 119 Sandgate Rd., Folkestone, Kent	Holidays	'Your Rights Over 60' 'Back to Work' etc.
TEAR Fund, 1 Bridgeman Rd., Teddington, Middlesex TW11 9AJ	Overseas relief	—
Women's Royal Voluntary Service, 17 Old Park Lane, London W1Y 4AJ	Welfare	—
Workers' Educational Association, 9 Upper Berkley St., London W1H 8BY	Education	—